The *Colours* *of* *Love*

RELATIONSHIP MANUAL

Gbengá & Selone Ajewolé

X I
PUBLISHING

Publisher: 29Eleven Publishing

Photography: Andrew Harahwa & Ebun Aleshe

Typesetting: Elaine Sharples

Book Cover Design: Heather UpChurch | Art & Design Studios

The Colours of Love is a division of 29Eleven Publishing

www.thecoloursoflove.co.uk

Distributed by 29Eleven Publishing

Scripture quotations are taken from:

The Holy Bible. New King James Version (NKJV)

Copyright @ 1982 by Thomas Nelson, Inc. All rights reserved.

The Holy Bible, New Living Translation (NLT) Copyright @ 1996.

Tyndale House Publishers, Inc.

The Holy Bible, English Standard Version (ESV) Copyright © 2001 Crossway, Good News Publishers.

The Holy Bible, New International Version ®, NIV® Copyright © 1973, 1978, 1984, 2011 by Biblica, Inc.® Used by permission. All rights reserved worldwide.

The Message. Copyright © 1993, 1994, 1995, 1996, 2000, 2001, 2002. Used by permission of NavPress Publishing Group.

ISBN: 978-0-9929960-0-0 paperback ·

ISBN: 978-0-9929960-1-7 eBook

To MARLENE + ANTHONY

We dedicate this book to The One Who is love, Who teaches us to love and Who showers us with His love – Jesus Christ!

To our mums, Janet & Antonia, and to our two precious sons, Aryeh & Asriel, we truly love you!

WE LOVE YOU GUYS MORE THAN YOU!

LOVE SELONE
+ PASTOR G
XXX

ENDORSEMENTS

Relationships can be the most amazing and fulfilling experiences in life or very complex and complicated realities. In order to maximize them there are key principles we all must learn, embrace and employ. The Colours of Love Relationship Manual concisely lays out these truths in practical and powerful ways. My dear friends, the Ajewolés do a masterful job at breaking down the keys on how to keep your love ablaze.

Touré Roberts,
Author, Speaker, Pastor, Humanitarian

The book "The Colours of Love" identifies how to have a healthy relationship by taking the reader through three simple to understand yet challenging and encouraging stages. This book will help many people regardless of their relationship status.

Dan Blythe,
Hillsong Church London

Pastor Gbenga and Selone Ajewolé have taken the time out to produce not just a book but also a resource that acts as a manual and guide at every stage of one's relationship. If you are single or at the friendship stage this is for you. If you are courting or engaged this is for you. If you are married this is for you. I commend the Ajewole's for taking the time to share the necessary tools, wisdom and principles to produce Godly relationships. I commend them on their transparency and desire to empower the individual to go deeper and explore what it means to walk in The Colours of Love. You will be blessed!

Kunlé Oyedeji,
The Cornerstone Ministry
Author, *Relationship Matters*

This is an excellent resource for singles, those who are courting, considering marriage or are married already. I've been going through much of this process in my own relationship and it's imperative that singles and couples know what to look for in the pursuit of a life mate. Thank you for making it plain!
Lauren Evans
Singer & Songwriter

Wow, I gained a lot from reading The Colours of Love Relationship Manual. There is a great deal of wisdom in each section. I really absorbed the wholesome, but completely real and honest insight presented. It was so refreshing to read about a couple that were friends, and then a committed couple who completely loved hanging out with each other, and actually enjoy being married!

Rachel Martin,
Humanitarian

ACKNOWLEDGMENTS

We have so many people to thank for their support in writing this book and are eternally grateful for their constant cheerleading in this process.

To our family and our family at The Rock Church, your prayers and encouragement have made this journey worthwhile.

Rachel Martin, our Aussie sister who sat through all the pages of the book to give us authentic and detailed feedback, your belief in us brought the book to life! We appreciate you more than you know.

To our dear friend, Lauren Evans who took time out from her world tour to look over the book and provide some amazing feedback. We are glad it resonated with you in such a powerful way! Thank you so much for taking time out for us. Send us some of that LA sunshine!

To some amazing Pastors in our lives: Kunle Oyedeji, Tim & Adwoa Ramsay and Dan Blythe. Thank you for taking the time out to read excerpts of the manual and for giving us your feedback promptly despite your very hectic schedules.

Pastor Touré Roberts, thank you for your support, love and faith in us throughout the writing process, and life in general.

A huge heartfelt thank-you to our adopted-father, 'Chief' aka Pastor Kolade Adebayo-Oke, who on a rainy autumn afternoon in 2007, presided over our marriage ceremony. We appreciate your prayers and for consistently being in our corner.

We love you guys, God bless you all real good!

CONTENTS

INTRODUCTION

I f you've picked up this book, chances are, you have some questions about the complex nature of relationships. Well, we are a young husband and wife team who have been happy together for what feels like a lifetime. We believe we have this thing called love mostly figured out and have decided to share some golden nuggets with you to help you in your quest for real, loving and forever lasting relationships.

After fourteen years of friendship, thirteen years as a couple and seven years as committed life partners, we feel that this is the right time to talk about how to thrive in a relationship, and be content with the person you were originally designed for. As the Lead and Executive Pastor at The Rock Church based in London, my husband (G) and I (Selone) have facilitated many pre-marital, marriage and relationship counselling sessions for people from all walks of life. They have found our advice and coaching to be invaluable to starting, fixing or simply maintaining a happy home. A Psychology degree, independent psychological research on love and post-graduate relationship counselling studies has further cemented our understanding of the field.

My husband and I are surrounded by a large network of people and have noticed over the years that collectively we have been a natural source that people gravitate towards for firm, frank but fair and understanding relationship advice. People have commented on their desire to be able to emulate the type of relationship that we have. They trust both our professional knowledge and personal experience, and believe that regardless of the nature of the issues they present, we will provide objective and accurate advice about how best to move forward. This is why we developed 'The Colours of Love' (TCOL) series: to provide answers for those who would like to know how to navigate the field of finding and maintaining loving, lasting relationships.

TCOL is therefore a multifaceted relationship enhancement service where we aim to help you unveil the true essence of love, while giving you the ingredients necessary to attain and maintain happy, healthy and fulfilling relationships. It consists of interactive Relationship Seminars & Workshops, Relationship and Marriage Counselling and more recently, this easy to read, straight to the point *The Colours of Love Relationship Manual*. The feedback received from running seminars across the country was that the information presented was extremely insightful and should be available for people to reflect on afterwards. As a result we developed the manual as a point of reference, which could be used to explore current situations, guide decision-making and challenge preconceived relationship ideologies.

We believe that the reason we are so happy together is because our love for one another is based upon Christian principles. This manual however, transcends all cultural and religious norms and has the ability to impart knowledge whether you sing in the choir or avoid religion like the plague! From reading this manual, we hope you will gain the insight, knowledge and practical advice you need to enhance your relationship or to equip you to make wiser relationship decisions in the future. Ultimately, we hope it will cause you to look deeply and objectively at how you relate to others and to think about how you can make positive changes within yourself, that will maximise your loving and partnership capabilities overall.

THE COLOURS OF LOVE DEFINED

We have created a concept using three colours (Red, Yellow & Green) to define and explore the three main stages of every romantic relationship; this is what we refer to as *'The Colours of Love'*. Below is an outline of the stage each colour represents:

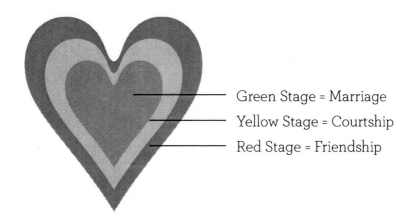

Green Stage = Marriage
Yellow Stage = Courtship
Red Stage = Friendship

Red Stage

Red is a bold, loud colour that makes a statement. The Red stage is the point at which individuals should **STOP** and think before entering into a relationship. It's the stage upon which individuals should seek to establish nothing more than the basis of a solid friendship.

Yellow Stage

Yellow is a warm colour that is used to represent the courtship stage of a relationship where two people are moving forward together at an appropriate pace towards marriage. It consists of getting to know each other more deeply after the friendship forged in the Red (friendship) stage and learning to proactively manage certain aspects of a relationship that can stop a couple progressing onto the Green (marriage) stage if left unchecked.

Green Stage

Green symbolises a state of peace and contentment most of the time. Despite the pressures of life, marriage should be a peaceful place, where the person who you have chosen to spend your life with is simply 'enough'. It is therefore the final stage where all couples should strive together to not only achieve, but also more importantly maintain since approximately forty percent of UK marriages in recent years have ended in divorce.

These colours represent the different stages of any romantic relationship and will be explored in more detail throughout the book. We understand that our readers might be at different stages of a relationship or not currently in a relationship at all. Either way, exploring these stages thoroughly will allow you to make changes for the better now or healthier choices in the future. So come with us on this journey, let us take you through, *'The Colours of Love'*.

Stage 1

RED (FRIENDSHIP)

When you think of the colour red in reference to relationships, what symbolism do you draw? Intense passion, powerful emotion or a compelling desire to love beyond measure? All of this may indeed be true but since it's open to subjective interpretation, we have chosen to look at this colour in a slightly different way. To us, just like the red light in a traffic light system, red screams 'WAIT, CAUTION and STOP!" The red stage is therefore the point at which we believe there are benefits to stopping and thinking BEFORE embarking on a new relationship.

Things to consider within this stage are:

- What is love to me?

- Why choose love?

- The importance of building a solid friendship first.

- Pre-Relationship red flags.

- When is it time to move forward?

During the next few chapters, lets unravel the thoughts of a good Red stage thinker!

Chapter One

LOVE IS...

From the psychological research we have undertaken about love, we have discovered a deep and compelling insight into this complex phenomenon. Romantic love is a human emotion that may be experienced by most individuals at some stage in their lives. Although romantic love is a familiar concept to most, Psychologists Beall and Sternberg (1995) highlight that social scientific literature seems to have difficulty in defining it appropriately. A vast amount of definitions have been posed, yet although fruitful, such approaches fail to capture the essence of the actual experiences of love. For this reason, Psychologists Sternberg and Grajek (1984) maintain, that even though love is an intense human emotion, no one quite knows exactly what it is.

"OK, so you are not going to give me a Psychological thesis on love are you?" we hear you wondering but don't tempt us, as our love for these theories run deep! Indulge us for a little while longer however, as these psychological aspects of love will help you to explore what love truly is to you.

So, back to the psycho-pop stuff we were talking about before, in order to help bring some clarity to what love really is, Sternberg (1986) proposed that love in the context of interpersonal relationships, could be conceptualised as consisting of three main components. He devised the *Triangular Theory of Love,* which he claims include an intimacy, passion and decision/commitment component. Sternberg highlights that intimacy encompasses feelings of closeness, attachment and the notion of being bonded with another person. Passion in contrast is the motivational component of love. It refers to drives that lead to romance, physical attraction and sexual consummation. Commitment is the cognitive controller (your brain) in a loving relationship. In the short term this involves a decision to accept such a relationship; the long-term aspect involves the commitment to maintain the relationship. According to Sternberg, the amount of love experienced, is therefore dependent upon the intensity of these three components, and also on the strength of each relative to the other. The strength of each component is subject to change over time as a romantic relationship matures. It is unlikely that a relationship based on one component, rather than all three will survive indefinitely. Are you with us so far? These three components can be combined to produce eight types of love.

Eight Types of Love

Type of Love	Intimacy	Passion	Commitment
Non Love (Not depicted on triangle)			
Liking/Friendship	✘		
Infatuation		✘	
Empty Love			✘
Romantic Love	✘	✘	
Companionate Love	✘		✘
Fatuous Love		✘	✘
Consummate Love	✘	✘	✘

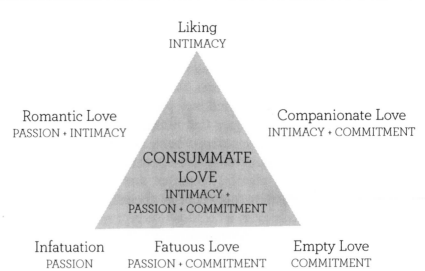

Liking
INTIMACY

Romantic Love
PASSION + INTIMACY

Companionate Love
INTIMACY + COMMITMENT

CONSUMMATE LOVE
INTIMACY + PASSION + COMMITMENT

Infatuation
PASSION

Fatuous Love
PASSION + COMMITMENT

Empty Love
COMMITMENT

Non-Love: You know the casual interaction that we have with others throughout everyday life? Well, that is what we call non-love. It is an absence of all three components of love.

Liking/Friendship: Ever had feelings of closeness and warmth but not feelings of passion or long-term commitment? This can be described as liking or friendship.

Infatuation: "He's so perfect, he could do no wrong in my eyes!" Are you sure? When infatuation arises it normally means that intimacy and commitment are lacking but passionate arousal is at the forefront. Romantic relationships often begin in this way and unless intimacy and commitment develop over time, this type of love tends to evaporate.

Empty Love: This is when it feels like there is not much left. It can be described as complete commitment with the absence of intimacy or passion. It can arise due to the deterioration of a solid love relationship, can blossom into another type of love and be built upon in situations such as arranged marriages. This suggests that empty love is not necessarily the terminal state of a long-term relationship, but it can actually be the beginning of one. Hope is therefore on the horizon!

Romantic Love: You know the type of lovers that tend to be physically and emotionally attracted to one another where they have an intimate and passionate type of bond but lack commitment? Well, this is the type of love we are describing here. Jennifer Lopez and Cris Judd who were married for a mere nine months should definitely spring to mind. Sorry Jenny!

Companionate Love: To experience this type of love usually suggests that although passion is lacking, intimacy and long-term commitment are the overriding aspects. This can often occur in long-term marriages where passion has run out of town but deep affection and commitment have settled in for good. This type of love can also be present within family members and very close and platonic friends.

Fatuous Love: Have you ever heard of couples that just begin dating and before you know it, they are married? Well, this is what we call fatuous love: where the commitment to one another is based upon the passion shared without the presence of, and time taken to grow intimate involvement.

Consummate Love: Now this is the type of love that most people strive for, it is what people usually describe when they talk about two people as being 'the perfect couple'. Features of consummate love include: long-term, passionate, exciting and fulfilling sex lives, being content with only their other half, easily managing the minimal disputes that do occur, and simply revelling in maintaining the relationship with each other. As great as this sounds, Sternberg highlights that maintaining this type of love could be harder than actually obtaining it in the first place. He believes that even the greatest love has the potential to die. For instance, if the passion deteriorates over time, it can change into companionate love therefore although idolised by many, this type of love may not be permanent.

In our life time and with different friends or partners, it is likely that one may experience some if not all of these types of love, even at different stages during one relationship. For many, the goal is to achieve consummate love, but what about you? Despite the attempts to highlight eight different definitions of love, your thoughts and feelings about it may not fit into any of these. What is love to you? To help you bring out your subjective thoughts on this complex phenomenon, we have a short exercise to allow you to explore ideas you may not have even realised you have.

This exercise will help you to begin exploring your thoughts not only about what love is, but also what it isn't. Read the following statements about love and put them into order in terms of how much you agree or disagree with them. The ranking values are +3 (Strongly Agree) to -3 (Strongly Disagree). There are seven statements and only one can be assigned to each ranking value.

For example:

You simply add the number of the statement you agree or disagree with in the box above the ranking value, e.g. one may believe statement number five least describes their ideology of love and as such you may put this above -3 (Strongly Disagree). You need to fill in all the boxes based in order of **what love is to you**. Please see the following example:

Romantic Love Is (Exercise example)

Statements:

"Romantic Love Is...."
1. Expressed ultimately by the commitment of marriage
2. Easiest to offer when personal needs are already cared for
3. An extension of platonic friendship
4. Requiring as little from your mate as possible
5. Mainly to do with physical attraction
6. Completely accepting your partner for the person that they are
7. The sharing of everyday problems

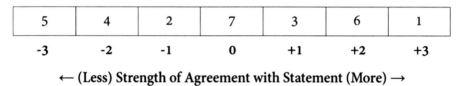

5	4	2	7	3	6	1
-3	-2	-1	0	+1	+2	+3

← (Less) Strength of Agreement with Statement (More) →

Romantic Love Is (Exercise)

Statements:

"Romantic Love Is...."
1. Expressed ultimately by the commitment of marriage
2. Easiest to offer when personal needs are already cared for
3. An extension of platonic friendship
4. Requiring as little from your mate as possible
5. Mainly to do with physical attraction
6. Completely accepting your partner for the person that they are
7. The sharing of everyday problems

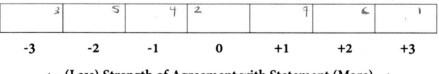

3	5	4	2		7	6	1
-3	-2	-1	0	+1	+2	+3	

← (Less) Strength of Agreement with Statement (More) →

However you see love, and whether you are in the Red, Yellow or Green stage, here are a few good ideas about what true love should encompass:

Love never gives up.
Love cares more for others than for self.
Love doesn't want what it doesn't have.
Love doesn't strut,
Doesn't have a swelled head,
Doesn't force itself on others,
Isn't always "me first,"
Doesn't fly off the handle,
Doesn't keep score of the sins of others,
Doesn't revel when others grovel,
Takes pleasure in the flowering of truth,
Puts up with anything,
Trusts God always,
Always looks for the best,
Never looks back,
But keeps going to the end.

(1 Corinthians 13:4-7 MSG)

If you want to make love last, make a conscious effort to love like this.

Chapter Two

WHY CHOOSE LOVE?

Then the Lord God said, "It is not good for the man to be alone, I will make a helper who is just right for him" (Genesis 2:18 NIV)

From the Christian perspective, God is the original designer of relationships and has highlighted that the purpose of a relationship is for us as individuals not to be by ourselves but rather to have a helpful partner who has been designed for us. It seems here that God advocates completely for relationships, and as He stated that He is making a "helper" rather than a "hinderer" who is just right for him, I doubt He intended this to mean drama filled, on and off, emotionally abusive, self-worth demolishing, "it's all about me", type of relationships! Whether you subscribe to the Christian faith or not, this is still a very good way of looking at love and relationships.

Before embarking on a romantic relationship, we believe it is important to only choose and create relationships that are purposeful. In order to achieve this, you first need to know the purpose romantic relationships serve.

The purpose of a relationship is:

- To have one special person to 'do life' with.

- To add value to your life.

- To have the support of another person with you while you pursue your dreams and aspirations.

The purpose of a relationship is not:

- To walk around with someone aesthetically pleasing on your arm.

- To spend the majority of your time together in disagreements or experiencing/administering physical or emotional abuse.

- Something that induces negative feelings the majority of the time and diminishes or is used to validate self worth.

- Something 'to do' because everyone else is doing it irrespective of whether it was actually a good idea to embark on a relationship at your present stage of life.

- To stroll nonchalantly through life with no goal in mind for yourself or your relationship.

Romantic relationships can therefore be very fulfilling adding a special dimension to your life that you would not be able to accomplish if you were on your own. It can also be the very thing that absorbs every bit of who you are, and drains you as a person, seeking to devour anything you have ever been or loved. The profound realisation of the real purpose of a relationship and applying this insight before investing in one (in the Red stage) will most definitely determine what type of relationship you create and in turn how sustainable it will be. Overall, adhering to these basic principles and considering the following question will save you a lot of wasted time and unnecessary heartache in the long run.

Why will/do you choose love?

I want to be (or am) in a relationship (either now or in the future) because:

Even if you are way past the Red stage, we implore you, from this very moment onwards: explore further, and digest thoroughly the original purpose of a relationship, and make future choices with this at the forefront of your mind.

"A relationship should enhance your life. If you could be happier on your own, what's the point?"

So, why choose love? You decide....

Chapter Three

SOLID FOUNDATIONS

In your lifetime you may have come across the analogy of the wise man that built his house upon a rock while the foolish man built his house upon sand. When the storm came into town, I bet you can guess which house remained standing. The sand man of course! OK, no, it was the rock man, we were just checking that you were paying attention. Anyway, as simple as this analogy is, deep and compelling insight can be drawn from it. This insight can be applied in a life changing, mindset altering way to the realm of relationships. If you hear nothing else from us in this manual (which we hope will not be the case) please hear this:

"Relationships that are not built with solid foundations seldom survive the small droplets of morning dew let alone the fierce and raging Hurricane Katrina's of this life. Build your house together upon solid rock and watch your relationship prevail against any storm"

That being said, let's explore how to build a solid foundation for a relationship that cannot be moved by light or ferocious winds. Believe it or not, the key to this is friendship. "Friendship? But that's boring!" Boring? That depends on who you're becoming friends with, and how much value you place on them as a person, as well us how much you truly desire for your relationship to last.

Let us break it down a little further. Friendship is a type of interpersonal relationship that is generally considered to be closer than association. It revolves around:

- Mutual compassion, trust and understanding.

- A tendency to desire the best for the other.

- An ability to lovingly speak the truth where necessary.

- Positive reciprocity (in essence, where both individuals give and receive mutually).

- Sympathy and empathy.

To begin a relationship as just friends, and taking the time to build on all of the attributes listed above, constitutes the solid foundation that should be developed in the Red stage. To have all of these things in place before becoming romantically involved, means that when difficult times arise, and believe us, they will, you are better equipped to handle them as you know each other deeply below the surface level and have built your house upon a rock.

Friends with benefits? Yes, there are some, but not in the way you may be thinking! Instead, the benefits of building a solid friendship with your potential mate are:

- Having someone to hang out with. This can include things such as going to the cinema or out to lunch providing you have enough money in the piggy bank.

- Learning how to communicate openly with another human being beyond social media.

- Accountability, which refers to having someone to pull you up when you make silly decisions.

- Learning new skills such as how to play Chess or budget your finances.

- Gaining inspiration and encouragement. This could involve someone knowing you are talented in song writing, inspiring you to write a song then commending your efforts and encouraging you to write more once you have finished.

- Knowing each other deeply as individuals and taking an interest in each other and everything that pertains to the both of you.

Without stating the obvious, a profound but often overlooked concept is: when you take time to develop a friendship first, you get to decide whether you actually LIKE the characteristics of this person BEFORE pursuing a romantic relationship.

"Can we be friends?" That's the question that G asked me over fourteen years ago. We met in a crammed and sweaty house party in North West London where garage tunes like *I'll Bring You Flowers* made it to number two in the UK Singles Chart and made you lose any decorum you had dancing crazy on the dusty brown carpet. Lets just say that after a few drinks being spilt and a rather tall person (him) leaning on a rather short person's head (me), we didn't get off to a very good start. Once we got passed the heated introductions, things began to seem a lot more positive. As we got to know each other more, he posed the question "Can we be friends?" We developed a solid and platonic friendship for a year before embarking on a relationship where I was able to see that I actually liked his company and the person I had grown to know.

In retrospect, that year of solid friendship is the foundation that has made G and I as strong as we are today. If anybody said "I saw G and he was wearing red socks!" I would categorically be able to refute that as I know him as a person and am clear that he is not too fond of red and would certainly never wear that colour, no, not even the Virgin Atlantic socks that come inside the complimentary toiletry pack presented to you on a transatlantic flight.

Being friends first helps you to get to know somebody at a deeper level. It should also, and has definitely been a place where the both of us felt comfortable enough to show ourselves undisguised. Ultimately though, within this friendship, the main thing that I have appreciated is that it has been enough to just be, well, me.

Friendship thoughts:

How important do you believe it is to build a solid foundation first? (*Please tick*)

Extremely Important ☐   Somewhat Important ☐

Not That Important ☐   Not Important At All ☐

Can you think of three reasons why you should invest in building a good friendship first?

1. ....

2. ....

3. ....

Can you think of any couples that you know or in the world of celebrities who have a solid and long lasting relationship because they built it upon friendship first?

1. ....

2. ....

3. ....

Solid foundations and friends with benefits, if you incorporate these principles into your Red stage thought processing, it's an idea we believe will allow you to win from here on out!

Chapter Four

RED FLAGS AND YELLOW CRAYONS

In a lot of situations there tends to be clear signs or signals about whether or not continuing to pursue a thing or person is actually a good idea. These are what we call *red flags*, which are in essence a warning sign that you should stop or at least consider stopping whatever it is you are about to move forward with. Problems arise when we ignore these signs because we really, really like the person or thing we are chasing, and become prepared to overlook it-for now. The main issue then becomes the 'for now'. Later on down the line, the very thing that we convinced ourselves was not a problem becomes the main bone of contention in our situation.

We believe that you don't have to experience something yourself in order to learn from it. If you see me jump into a puddle and get wet (Wellington boots or not) you don't also need to jump into it to know that the same will happen to you. Listen carefully to the examples we are sharing within this manual, as it will save you a lot of unnecessary pain in the long run. So before moving forward, let's consider a few puddles to watch out for, in essence, these are Pre-Relationship red flags:

Pre-Relationship red flags for men:

- **She is too needy:** Needy women tend to require your attention and constant affirmation, morning, noon and night. If she doesn't get what she needs from you exactly when she needs it, you run the risk of either all hell breaking loose, or her retreating further into a shell. A relationship with this type of woman will drain more of your time and energy than a good relationship should. We talked earlier about positive reciprocity where giving and taking is mutual, in this case, it would be very one sided and definitely not in your favour.

- **She is overtly sexy:** Picture this: a banging body, super tight stop you breathing type of clothing, twenty-four inch Indian Remy Straight Weave (colour 1b), a face full of make up with false fluttering eyelashes to match, cleavage from here to Spain and lastly those super long false nails that hinder her from picking up any coins that drop on the floor while she runs to the corner shop for milk on a Sunday morning. You may laugh, but for some ladies, this is their reality and to a lot of men, this is the epitome of beauty. Each to their own and admittedly, this overtly sexy dress code and flirtatious manor may not be a problem now, but could you introduce her to your mum and take her to family functions? Would you be proud to introduce her to the world as your wife?

- **She has no dreams and aspirations:** What is her ultimate goal in life? To be your trophy wife and to ride on your coattail? To watch and wait patiently while you pursue all you were designed for with the expectation that you will provide for her every need? G and I both have separate and joint dreams and aspirations that we actively pursue, and we push each other forward at each hurdle we face. Some people believe we need to slow down, but our goal is to ultimately leave a very positive legacy and to impact the world in a mighty way. That being said, we have no choice but to chase our dreams, this notion of dream chasing within each other is a very attractive quality, which has kept us as fresh and active as we are now, fourteen years on. Is it important to you for her to at least have her own dream?

- **She speaks negative words into my life:** It may come from a good place, as in she see's your potential and is trying to get you to recognise it. It's not necessarily what she says but rather how she says it. Instead of "Why can't you ever finish anything you start?!" she could consider "Hey babes, I see so much potential in you and I'm very proud of the work you have completed on the project thus far. I believe in your ability to excel and really want you to finish and finish well, so I just want to know if there is anything I can do to help you accomplish what you set out to achieve?" OK, so the second version is slightly long winded, but you get the idea. You need someone who can encourage you and push you forward rather than tear you down.

- **She offers but never ACTUALLY pays for dinner:** Over the past few years there has been a rise in the notion that men and women are to be seen as equal in all situations, except for some people, this excludes those that involve the woman parting with hard earned cash. For me however it has always been different. Even back in the day when I was at college with my £30 a week EMA money (student government allowance) and G had more money than I did, I would still offer and when accepted, I would pay for our meal. Further down the line in our relationship, things like this just became 50:50. I was happy to share what I had with him and he was with me. Typical gender roles went out of the window in our relationship a long time ago and have never resided here again. When you love someone, you both want to do nice things for each other, even if it means you're going to be slightly out of pocket. Be it McDonalds Happy Meals all around or an expensive dinner at The Ivy, this aspect of friendships or relationships should be mutual.

- **She is from a culture that may cause problems for me later down the line:** This is a tough one and is something we will explore in a lot more detail further on in the manual. If we look back throughout history there are many stories of cultures clashing and forbidding individuals to intermarry even when they are of the same race but are simply from a different region or tribe. This may not be an issue for you, but it may be for your family. Before moving forward, you need to decide irrespective of culture and tradition, how much weight you are willing to put on the opinions of others when making important decisions for your life, the life my friend, that only you can live.

Pre-Relationship red flags for women:

- **He is not a good friend:** Ladies, there are some guys that we find ourselves really attracted to on a physical level, but as we get to know them more deeply we realise that this is precisely where it stops. Good looks are great but the reality is they only last for a time and looking longingly into his eyes without a good and solid friendship will begin to wear its course. Does he make you laugh? Can you tell him anything? What's his favourite colour? Does he know yours? Would he willingly support you emotionally when you need it? Does he have the capacity to? Is he trustworthy? As previously noted, solid friendships are key to relationships flourishing and surviving, you just need to figure out if you can build one with him.

- **He is more interested in my body than in my mind:** We all know guys like this; all they desire from you is the physical. You need to question however if that's all you have on display. Have you showcased your mind rather than your extremely perky double D's? If you have, does he appear uninterested in anything other than your physical beauty? Again, you need to ask yourself specific questions, as once gravity begins to take hold; you want to be sure that he will still be inclined to stick around.

- **He is very giving, just not with his time:** Ever come across those guys that believe that they can substitute their time and attention with gift giving of some type? With all the will in the world, I have never known it possible for a Birkin (or Primark) bag to be able to console a person when they are feeling sad. Investing money is way less important than an investment of self and time.

- **He is not husband and father material:** If not, then, what's the point? Life's too short for meantime relationships. We believe that if you cannot see yourself long term with this person, raising a family with everything or nothing, you are definitely wasting time and energy that could better be spent on other areas of your life.

- **We don't have the same spiritual and religious views:** This is again such a sensitive topic, which can either cause you to stay together or part ways. We are not saying that it is impossible for a friendship or relationship to work when two people have opposing spiritual and religious beliefs, we are just saying that the road together is generally a lot smoother if you do. This will be explored in much more detail within the Yellow Stage.

- **I like him more than he likes me:** This seldom ends well. If ever you are in a situation where you feel more for someone than they feel for you, feelings of insecurity and inadequacy will always fester and will in time cause multiple problems. We don't suggest you move forward unless the feelings towards each other are mutual.

Seem extreme? Trust us, it's not. This is not even an exhaustive list; there are many more things you need to look out for! Also, in most cases these red flags can apply to both genders, well, apart from the line about the *perky double D's* of course! We know that perfection is something that the average human being is not capable of attaining, however, if the red flags outweigh the good qualities, we believe you need to reconsider whether pursuing a romantic relationship with this person is actually a good idea.

"He's cool but there are quite a few things about him that I need to work on changing." If we had a pound for every time we heard that, we could retire today! This is a prime example of people seeing the red flags, categorically ignoring them, moving forward with the relationship and thinking they are ready for the challenge of moulding someone, into the person they *want* them to be. If you are not perfect then don't make your life's mission into trying to make someone else perfect. Either accept them as they are with all those red flags flying around in the wind, or politely keep it moving.

Now take a moment to think about and write down five red flags that you can see in hindsight from past relationships, things that concern you about the relationship you may be about to enter into, or the relationship you are already in.

Five red flags right before my eyes:

1. ....

2. ....

3. ....

4. ....

5. ....

Once you have written them down, if you are about to be or are already in a relationship, you need to be honest enough to consider the severity of each red flag and whether continuing on in the same fashion is a good idea. If your red flags are from a past relationship, you need to think about whether you noticed and overlooked it before the relationship began or whether it has just become crystal clear to you in retrospect. Think about whether you feel these contributed to the dissolution of your relationship and then celebrate your growth and learn from your experience.

OK, so now we have discussed all things 'Red' and you should have a clearer understanding of what to do and consider **BEFORE** you enter a relationship. It is important to condense this Red stage reasoning into a few profound and interesting points for you to refer back to when you feel the need. First, stop and think before entering a relationship and ask yourself the following questions:

- What is love to me? Do we think about love in a similar way? Are we compatible in terms of our ideologies of love?

- What's the purpose of a relationship, and what value would one add to my life? Even though everybody else seems to be doing it, am I ready for one now?

- Does he or she want to be my friend first or just my lover straight away?

- Am I ignoring clear signs that this isn't a great idea? Have I sought counsel from the people that care for me and give good advice?

- Do I understand that if I don't stop and think before I enter a relationship, I may be wasting time I can never get back?

Ponder on these things, then, if everything is in order and you are ready to move forward, put your red crayon down, get a piece of paper big enough for the two of you to share and use your yellow crayons to sketch a joint masterpiece.

Stage 2

YELLOW (COURTSHIP)

If you think of the colours that make up a warm summers day, the colour yellow would more than likely feature somewhere in the scene. If you live in England, warm sunny days are few and far between, and even though we crave the heat so much, sometimes the temperature becomes unsuitable for our particular needs. We often want it to be hot, just not too hot and would love to be able to adjust the temperature of the heat so that it does not become unbearable. The same can be said for relationships whereby in the Yellow stage (courtship), we need to control the climate as it were, otherwise progression to the Green stage (marriage) becomes increasingly unlikely. The Yellow stage is the courtship segment of a relationship where two people are pacing themselves steadily towards marriage, seeking to manage and eliminate any threats to their future dream of being together forever. In order to progress to the Green stage or at best remain content in the Yellow stage, you need to be aware of and consistently work on a number of factors. These include, but are not limited to:

- Clearly outlining whether or not you have moved from friendship into courtship.

- Communication.

- Conflict management.

- Investing in sorting out any emotional baggage, problems with spiritual unity and being mindful of the time and commitment required to make a relationship work.

- Considering balance, respect and maintaining physical attraction.

- Cultural and family expectations.

- Understanding the benefits of abstinence until marriage.

- All the things to consider before making a life long commitment and saying "I do."

Yellow crayons at the ready? Let's explore this further.

Chapter Five

ARE WE COURTING?

"Are you guys together?"

"Us? No, um, we're just friends, well, kind of. Ugh! We don't really know, like my Facebook page says: It's complicated!"

People who have crossed over from being friends into romantic partners, or from the Red into the Yellow stage without realising it often have trouble answering this question. The way to gauge if a friendship between a male and a female has blossomed, or at least on the way to developing into something more, is to ask the people involved the following questions:

- What if he or she was to begin pursuing another relationship during this time, how would you feel? Hurt or jealous?

- Even if it is an unwritten or unspoken rule, do you just expect him or her to 'know' that from this point onwards, they should only have eyes for you?

- Do you spend more time with this individual either in person or on the phone than you do with anyone else?

- Have your family or friends become accustomed to knowing that this person is a major part of your life, whether they see him or her often, or have to endure endless hours of you going on about them like a kid excited about tomorrows trip to Disneyland?

- Are you catching feelings?

- Could it be possible that you are actually in a relationship but are both yet to realise it or define it?

It was for us. After well over a year of friendship there were blatant signs that we had become more than friends. These included but were not limited to:

- Me taking G and only G to all family functions.

- Us talking about each other non-stop to anyone that would listen.

- Us talking to each other for a minimum of what felt like one million times a day.

- Us making the long trip between South London to North West London more often than a friend would.

- Us going on many 'outings' to places like parties or the cinema together.

- Both of our sets of friends becoming naturally affiliated with one another.

- Us assigning special ringtones for each other such as a slow jam called *My Whole Life Has Changed* by Ginuwine. It got to the point where my mum started to make up her own lyrics to the song because it rang way more than any other ringtone on my phone!

Despite all of these signs, it took my brother in law to sit me down and tell me that we had in fact crossed over into boyfriend and girlfriend territory! To everyone else, it was crystal clear that we had become more than friends. To us, and maybe more to me, there was a hesitance around making things official. My concerns about this surrounded the fact that even though we had been building this friendship for over a year, I had not too long come out of another relationship. It was also about having to take on the responsibility of being someone's partner, and wondering if I was ready to hold someone else's heart in my hand again. Lastly, it was the fear of wondering whether we had put enough in at this point to begin a relationship that would last the distance. After many lengthy talks together around the subject of an exclusive romantic relationship between the two of us, detailing lovingly the pace at which we were both comfortable taking, we decided to define ourselves as being in a partnership that wasn't just for the meantime, one that would require extra care and attention for it to blossom into what it is today. Can you relate? It's possible that if not now, there has been or will be one stage in the future where you will.

The reason why we posed the question as "Are we courting?" rather than

"Are we dating?" is because of the stark contrast and subsequent connotations that can be drawn from their distinct definitions:

Courting:

To be involved with someone romantically, typically with the intention of marrying. It is also the act, period, or art of seeking the love of someone with intent to marry.

Dating:

The definition of dating varies around the world but it most commonly involves two people trying out a relationship, and exploring levels of compatibility by going out together as a couple in public.

To us, dating is simply a cheap imitation of courting. We know that courting sounds like a really old-fashioned word, but since dating is a time to 'see' if they would work well as a couple, there is an opportunity here to behave like one in certain aspects (e.g. sexual relations) and then decide that because they were simply dating, if things are not working out, no further long-term work or commitment is required. These things can happen within courtship, however, based on the fact that there is an 'intent to marry', the casual "I can clock out at the drop of a hat if I choose to" element should be eradicated. As previously stated we believe that the Red or friendship stage is where you should do most of the ground work to ascertain whether or not you are compatible and then leave the Yellow or courtship stage to build upon the common ground you have already established.

It is clear, therefore, that sometimes you can move from a Red to Yellow stage, or friendship to courtship without knowing it while being blinded by the beauty of your potential mate. If you think you may have crossed over into a relationship, take a moment to reflect on the aforementioned information and discuss these at length with your potential partner. You both need to stand back and objectively think about at least five signs that could suggest that you have transitioned into being a couple without realising it. If you are not in a relationship at the moment, think about and note down five signs not already listed for you to watch out for to prevent unconsciously moving onto relationship status.

Are we courting? Five possible signs that we are:

1. ....

2. ....

3. ....

4. ....

5. ....

Are we courting? You both need to decide.

Chapter Six

TWO EARS AND ONE MOUTH

One of the most undervalued and often overlooked components of a relationship is communication. A fundamental part of any healthy partnership is good communication! Whenever a couple fail to communicate effectively and respectfully, this will have an adverse affect on their ability to relate to each other, trust each other and feel loved within the confines of their special bond. Ultimately this will lead to a disconnection between the couple, and a relationship lacking in good communication seldom survives. With all the pressures, anxieties, expectations, and curveballs that a couple experience, developing and consistently practicing good communication assists, but does not necessarily ensure the survival of a potentially doomed relationship. The reason good communication alone cannot ensure a relationship will survive is because there are several other factors to consider within the Yellow stage; good communication, however, is a very important component that is not to be ignored.

Oftentimes, in our experience coaching couples, one thing that constantly comes up in the breakdown of a relationship, is their inability to communicate. "My partner simply doesn't listen!" is a phrase both parties often use to apportion blame elsewhere. In responding to this, the simplest illustration to give is that we are created with one mouth and two ears, and we should use them in that ratio of two to one. When we are able to develop this discipline: listening twice as much as we talk, it makes for better communication, as the other person will feel that their thoughts, concerns, fears, and emotions are being taken seriously. Selone has learnt more about this during her postgraduate counselling placement, where she described having to fight the urge to finish her client's sentence, and actively listen to what *they* have to say; rather than pre-empting what she thinks they are going to, or should say. It is not an easy discipline to master, but it is one that adds value to any relationship once you do.

When we think about communication, we often think about it in a verbal sense. You may be surprised to know, however, that in any relationship, most of what we actually mean or want to say is carried out by the unspoken words, which manifests itself in our body language, facial expressions, and behaviour. In actual fact, ninety-three percent of our communication is non-verbal, meaning that the actual words that come out of our mouth only make up seven percent of our communication. Of the ninety-three percent of non-verbal communication, thirty-eight percent is constituted of vocals, which comprises the volume, pitch, rhythm, and tone of what is being said. Most of us are familiar with the statement **"It's not what was said, but *how* it was said!"** Body movements, including facial expressions are said to make up the other fifty-five percent of non-verbal communication. Knowing these facts, it's no wonder people draw correct or incorrect conclusions about the intention behind a phrase because of how it was said. This is even true of an employee and manager relationship. If for example your manager said, "Rebecca, can you come into my office please as I need to have a word with you", you may find yourself trying to dissect whether they are calling you in for a promotion, or to dismiss you, simply based upon the non-verbal cues given. Our non-verbal communication therefore, may warrant more attention than we currently give it. This will ensure that our partner does not draw the wrong conclusions about what we are attempting to convey, thereby lessening the chance that an argument or disagreement will blow up further than it needed to.

Most relationships experience difficulties, often because of a couple's inability to communicate concisely, respectfully, clearly, and honestly. Therefore, the majority of the time, especially when discussing situations that have the potential to become heated, verbal communication within a relationship, needs to be clear and concise, supported by a positive, respectful and considerate non-verbal demeanour. Are we suggesting you should smile and be all 'lovey-dovey' during a disagreement? No, that would be unrealistic and may be misinterpreted as you not taking the moment seriously. We are highlighting, however, that the damage done could be a lot less if you consider these things, and make a decision to be 'slow to anger' in the first instance.

It is during the Yellow, courtship stage then, that a couple must really work on what it means to be an effective communicator, and understand what is required to lovingly communicate their feelings, thoughts, and emotions, with their partner, without sabotaging and wrecking their relationship. Couples in the courtship stage must realise that words have great power, and can either breathe life and encouragement into a relationship, or alternatively can destroy and take the wind out of the sail of their partner.

One of the greatest lies ever told, is found in the statement "Sticks and stones may break my bones, but words can never hurt me." In reality, for anyone who has ever been on the receiving end of very harsh, negative and hurtful words, we know that they have the propensity to reach deep into our soul, and cause us to doubt ourselves, our abilities, our value and feel a sense of rejection and betrayal. In order to build and sustain a relationship, a couple must pay close attention to all the verbal and non-verbal expressions they exude.

Solomon, the wisest man to have ever lived gives us an insight of the power of words when he said: *The tongue can bring death or life; those who love to talk will reap the consequences* (Proverbs 18:21 NLT). In essence, Solomon enables us to understand that words have the power to either give life to a situation, or bring death to it. Whichever you choose will have a massive affect on the fruits you are able to produce, which will either be good or bad or even happy or sad in relation to the person who has received the words uttered. There will be instances where you will need to tell a person you love the truth about a situation or choice they have made, but this must be done tactfully using your tongue to breath life, hope and renewed perspective.

It is also important that in the heat of the moment, and under great external pressures, couples must learn to be disciplined enough to ensure that destructive words are never uttered. Once words leave our mouths, they can never be retracted. Unlike words constructed on a computer, once a word has been uttered, there is no 'undo' button to erase what has already been said.

Below are some simple principles that all couples should strive to adhere to that can ensure they are practicing effective and loving communication:

- **Choose the right time**: Believe it or not, timing is everything. In our own relationship, we are mindful of choosing the right time to talk about very serious matters, in an environment of fun or relaxation. We recognised early in our relationship that it is not a good idea to talk about something extremely serious, when we have just finished a long day at the office or are struggling from a lack of sleep, and are more likely to be easily irritated. We often choose to talk about very serious matters, maybe while watching a film in the living room, or going on a nature walk while our eldest son almost steers his bike into every passing person or tree. Choosing a time when we are both in a relaxed mood minimises the tension, as we are both chilled and more receptive. It's also advisable not to have serious conversations when one or both of you are under external pressures, or rushing out the door to catch the late train to work.

- **Develop a pleasant tone:** As mentioned earlier in this chapter, sometimes, it's not what has been said that leads to a disconnection or escalates a situation, but rather the way it has been said. Therefore, it's important even in the courtship stage that a couple learns to develop a tone that still says, "I love you, I respect you, I trust you and I honour you." You don't want to be known as the nagging partner with the 'horrible high pitched, condescending, everyone shudders when they hear you talk, and runs in the other direction' type of tone. Ensuring that voices are not raised during a discussion helps with this also.

- **Be clear and specific.** It is important that things are not miscommunicated or misunderstood during a conversation. Therefore, it is vital that communication is clear, specific and above all, easily understood. A healthy relationship requires that a couple strives to make dialogue explicit, and that whatever they are communicating is what they really feel. It is unrealistic to believe our needs will be met if we are not honest and clear about what we are experiencing inside. We must ensure that we do not make assumptions that our significant other has understood what is required. Rather, the couple should strive to conclude their conversation by asking each other what they believe is being asked/required of them to ensure they have a good grasp of what was uttered. Being clear and specific also ensures that nothing is lost in translation. Remember, your partner is not a mind reader and you may need to fill in between the lines to make sure they get your point.

- **Be positive:** Always strive to put a positive or even, humorous spin on any conversation. This will help create a positive and supportive atmosphere, which will hopefully avoid either of you having their backs up against the wall, and becoming defensive.

- **Be courteous and respectful of your mate's opinion:** There's nothing worse than being made to feel as if your opinion, feelings, concerns, or thoughts are unimportant in any arena of life. A relationship is the place you should feel safest, and it should allow you to be at your most vulnerable without fear of rejection or disrespect. This is why listening is key. Actively listening will reassure your partner that he/she has a say in the relationship, and is valued and respected in your partnership. Being patient and not jumping in every few seconds, shows that you are actually interested in what your mate has to say.

- **Be sensitive to the needs and feelings of your partner:** This is all about acknowledging that your partner has needs, respecting their individuality and allowing them to express themselves freely. A healthy relationship builds a 'safe zone', which liberates both partners to feel that, their needs and feelings are important to their partner. Developing the discipline of communicating well will ensure that both partners can conclude a conversation or discussion, knowing that they are still respected, and their feelings are valued.

- **Work together to develop the art of conversation:** It has often been said that good, effective communication is an art form. A couple should strategically and purposefully try to perfect the art of communication at every opportunity presented to them, consistently showing respect, listening more than they talk (two ears, one mouth), watching the tone and body language used, showing interest in what the other person is saying, or not saying, and seeking to address this lovingly.

- **Comfortable silence:** Be comfortable enough to sit silently beside each other, without the need to fill the space with empty words or feeling the need to force your partner into saying something when they are still processing what has been presented to them. In an extremely noisy world, sometimes silence is like music to the soul.

Over the years, we have developed the ability to communicate with each other without words. As a mater of fact, we can actually be in a room that is full of other people, and be able to say one thousand things to each other without speaking or uttering a word, especially when someone's choice of shoes is not very well matched to their suit. This is something every couple should strive for, as it enables the couple to read each other's moods, and emotions without words ever being said.

So how do we learn to listen? It might seem like a no brainer but it simply includes things like:

- Giving good eye contact.

- Sitting attentively.

- Acting and being genuinely interested.

- Adding appropriate phrases to show agreement, interest or understanding. This however, does not include grunting!

- Asking well thought out questions to seek clarity.

- When you think your partner is finished talking, listen a little longer.

As human beings that are not infallible, it would be impossible to get one hundred percent of this right all of the time. If however the majority of the time you can incorporate at least some of these skills, your relationship will be a much happier place to live while you navigate your way through the Yellow stage. Two ears and one mouth, what's the ratio in your relationship?

Chapter Seven

BOXING GLOVES

Another vital aspect to learn about within the Yellow stage is how to cultivate and develop the discipline of conflict management. Too often, couples only learn the need for conflict management while picking up the messy residue, and debris left after a catastrophic conflict. However, it is wiser to possess the tools and understanding of resolving relationship conflicts way before they creep up on you.

No matter how perfect a relationship appears to be, every relationship experiences conflict, even ours! Every couple will go through challenging times, whereby they disagree on certain issues, they get on each other's last nerve and they rub each other up the wrong way. Yes, even we go through conflicts where we are ready to fight to the finish to ensure we get our points across, where I want my wife to know that I'm in the right and want to ensure that my Nigerian and South London crafted tenor voice is heard! This seldom ends well though, thus we have learnt how to 'box' a bit more effectively.

No two people will ever agree on everything all the time. No matter how madly in love you are with your 'boo', you won't always agree! Knowing this from the beginning will stop one trying to ensure that everyday is perfect and all opinions are in sync as this is just not reality. In such a big world we all have our own unique identity. With these individual ways of interacting, thinking and behaving, at one point or another, conflict will happen.

There are a few reasons why conflict arises in relationships. These include, but are not limited to:

- Misunderstood or unclear communication.

- Differences of opinion on a particular subject.

- A desire to be right all the time.

- A person sugar coating how they really feel about a topic or situation.

- External pressures such as financial strain, a lack of job security and the like.

- Seeking to be the dominant partner (not a good relationship to be in!).

- Having a strong emotional connection with someone and loving them almost too hard, which manifests itself in unpleasant ways.

The goal of conflict resolution within the context of a loving relationship is never to 'have one over' your partner, or to 'tweet' the fact that you've just shown your partner that 'you are in control' in the relationship. It should always be to arrive at a place of mutual agreement, understanding and still be in a loving relationship at the end of it all! We've witnessed too many couples who are so determined to prove themselves right, to show they are the 'alpha male', and in some cases the 'alpha female', that they will say anything or do anything to be proven right; irrespective of the collateral damage they cause. When some couples engage in a conflict, it feels and looks like a civil war. A war in which anything goes, very creative and hurtful words are delivered, past failings are dug up and thrown in the face of the one you supposedly love, couples dig deep to revive and resuscitate every negative attribute of their partner, and even more unfortunately in some cases, physical violence occurs. This type of relationship can easily lead to someone having to be buried six feet under and the other, serving life in prison. So getting this right now, is of utmost importance.

Conflict in and of itself is not a bad thing (as long as it doesn't result in broken glass and blue flashing lights outside your window). If the couple are intentional about working through the conflict, it can actually lead to growth, if they are respectful to each other through the way they communicate their grievances, and exercise positive actions to resolve them. Conflicts can either be the cause of frustration, anger, and resentment, or they can actually be the very tools that strengthen a relationship, helping it to grow to a whole new level. This depends on how willing each person is to humble themselves and find a good compromise after the disagreement.

One of the tricks we've learnt over the years is that there is always a middle ground, and room to compromise during a conflict, so that we can both feel victorious and vindicated at the end of a disagreement, without spilling any 'relational blood'. From the outset, we found it useful to establish some ground rules on how we would resolve disagreements and conflicts. Here are some examples of ground rules that we feel have helped prevent and manage conflict in our relationship:

- Primarily, we have Christ at the core of our relationship, and we understand that we are both a gift from Him. Therefore, no matter what, we must honour God's gifts.

- Secondly, we decided that breaking up in the Yellow stage (courtship) of our relationship, or divorce in the Green stage (our marriage) would not be an option. As such, we must constantly work to cultivate an atmosphere of love, where we both know that we are in each other's corner for life, even when we don't see eye to eye.

- We also promised each other right from the start, that we would never use any derogatory words towards each other. We had seen what havoc this lack of respect had wreaked on the relationships around us and wanted no part in it. Remember, our desire is to remain married and madly in love with each other even after we've had a fall out. Therefore, we understand that we can never use words or say things that will make us doubt or question our love and respect for each other once the dust has settled. This has been the saving grace for us never going too far in a disagreement and is one of the reasons why we are as happy and content as we are today.

In the heat of the moment, we can all say things that will likely hurt our partner's feelings, leaving them emotionally drained and betrayed. Therefore it is vital, if your desire is to safeguard your relationship that you respond to the situation rather than reacting to it! Take a moment to stop and think before you speak, and ensure you use phrases that don't 'accuse' or 'put down' your partner.

When managing or resolving conflict, applying simple principles such as using 'I' phrases rather than 'You' phrases can literally save your relationship and afford you the luxury to fall asleep on the sofa with both eyes closed. 'I' phrases deflect accusation and do not come across as offensive to the receiver. Take the following as an example: **"You are always home late!"** can easily turn into a full blown fight, whereas **"I get worried when you come home late, as I don't know what might have happened to** you", shows a concerned, caring, loving approach to basically the same statement. It is important also to focus only on the topic at hand, rather than digging up previous 'sins' or reminding your partner what he or she did last summer! Nothing will be resolved if previous issues are constantly being brought to the table in a vindictive manor. A truly loving and forgiving relationship should not keep a record of previous hurts and disappointments. Once you forgive, let it go! Unforgiveness is more poisonous to the victim than the original perpetrator.

If either of you feel you are too tense, upset or angry to continue with the conflict resolution, it is better to, take some time to cool off, and maybe reschedule for another time. The purpose of resolving the conflict is not to force your point across, or on the flip side, to keep quiet, refusing to utter anything. If you consider yourself to be grown up enough to enter into a relationship, then you must be grown up enough to communicate effectively and resolve conflicts effectively as a mature adult.

The following are some other tips to help you resolve and manage conflicts within your relationship more effectively:

- Be balanced in your approach, always keeping love, honour and respect at the forefront.

- Decide whether the issue at hand is even worth the amount of energy it's draining from the both of you. Ask yourself whether or not the issue is important enough for a conflict to arise in the first place. At times, couples argue over small issues that can be easily resolved by literally agreeing to disagree.

- 'Tomorrow' is a promise for no one, therefore, pride must be put aside, and you must not allow the sun to set on your anger. This is a Biblical gem that can do a whole lot of good for your relationship. Regardless of who is to blame, both parties within a relationship must be quick to simply say, " I'm sorry", forgive each other, and keep on moving forward in love.

- Restaurants are an amazing place to resolve conflicts. There are no opportunities to shout or explode in a public place, unless you want to spend the night in a jail cell. If you truly desire to resolve a conflict and deal with a niggling issue, book a table at a classy restaurant and start talking! KFC, McDonalds and the Burger King in Brixton tend to allow shouting so these do not count! Be creative!

- No shouting or swearing!

- Be polite and respectful at all times.

- Find a time when there are no other external problems likely to cause more irritation or anger, such as a recent job loss, loss of a family member, that time of the month (ladies only!) or even an episode of 'man flu'.

- Constantly offer affirmation and validation. Even though as a couple, you might disagree, it is reassuring to validate and protect each other's feelings.

- Under no circumstances should there be any insults or a desire to shame or belittle each other.

Despite the façade and the pumped out chests, a true loving couple, even in the midst of a conflict find it extremely difficult, lonely and painful not having their partner and best friend in their corner. Keep this in mind whenever you're upset with each other or making attempts to talk about a very difficult and draining issue.

One thing to bear in mind is that as men and women, our conflict resolution styles are drastically different. In most cases, but not all, women prefer to talk about a problem, and won't stop until their man is ready to talk about it too. Us men would rather resolve the issue in our minds first, get down to the park and have a shoot around on the basketball court or get to the gym and take out our frustration on the bench press. Women have a tendency to want to iron out the issue, making sure every niggling crease is ironed out. On the flip side, men are mostly 'happy go lucky' and even if there are underlying issues, we tend to be able to live with it. We would rather bring out the ironing board and iron a thousand shirts than sit down to iron out a problem with our partners. Despite these differences, a good couple will seek to figure out a conflict resolution style that works for 'them'.

Therefore, it is critical that each person learns to manage conflict correctly in order to enjoy a life-long, healthy and loving relationship. Conflicts should never be avoided, as oftentimes, issues will simmer under the surface, until they explode, with even more damaging and prolonged consequences. Instead, as it does arise, use these tools to manage conflicts, together. When approached correctly, you wont hopefully need actual boxing gloves!

Chapter Eight

JOINT PIGGY BANK

Being in a relationship is always going to cost you something! However, the return you get depends on how much you *and* your partner are willing to invest. When depositing pieces of oneself into a joint piggy bank on a regular basis, one must be aware that the statement 'The greater the investment, the higher the return' is only true if the amount invested is reciprocal. For the purposes of the Yellow stage, we will examine investment in regards to time and commitment, sorting through any emotional baggage and investing in the importance of spiritual harmony within your relationship.

Say, for example, Sue had just given birth to her third son, was feeling frumpy, and had set a goal to loose ten pounds within six months as she would be the Chief Bridesmaid at her best friends wedding. Sue decided to commit to exercising four days a week and eating healthy every day, irrespective of the sleepless nights and all her other responsibilities as a Mum. If for whatever reason she did not commit fully to either one of these tasks, the likelihood of her being able to reach the goal is reduced, and the fear of being the only 'out-of-shape' bridesmaid, would become more of a possibility. Put simply, in most cases, commitment leads to achievement.

The same can be said of relationships. When two people give their all without reserve, it helps to build feelings of security and is often equated with the notion of true love. During the Yellow stage it is important to look at how much each partner is investing, and how committed they are to the relationship. Problems will always arise when the commitment level within a relationship seems to be somewhat lopsided. It can be as simple as one person always being more willing than the other to cancel prior engagements in order to spend quality time with their partner. A lack of commitment can lead to uncertainty about the amount of value that is placed on the relationship and whether or not it can continue in this fashion. Investing wisely, therefore, by way of time and commitment is of utmost importance.

In addition, when talking about investment, some people forget to, or place little value on, properly dealing with previous emotional baggage. Imagine a man on the platform at Kings Cross International train station, ready to board the Eurostar to Paris with his new love that has just come down from Leeds to meet him. They are excited about their journey ahead and she jumps off of her train, ready to embrace him wholeheartedly, except she can't, because he is holding too many bags. With lots of baggage from previous relationships, it makes it hard to embrace each other and move forward. Forms of emotional baggage may include but are not limited to:

- Abuse
- Relationship scars
- Unresolved relationships
- Fear
- Poor relationship examples
- Self esteem issues

Investing in tackling emotional baggage by way of counselling or speaking with trusted friends before entering a new relationship is the best approach to this. It is important to get over one relationship and make time to self reflect on what went wrong, to ensure you don't make the same mistakes again, before starting another one. As long as you make future decisions with better clarity, you can to a degree prevent things from going wrong again, and you no longer need to be held hostage or paralysed with fear that the same issues and mistakes will be repeated. If, however, you have already found yourself in the Yellow stage having not dealt with any emotional baggage, and you don't want it to get in the way of your new relationship, pause for a moment, invest money, time and whatever you need to in order to deal with any emotional baggage you may have.

Lastly when looking at investment, it is important to consider how you will approach the spiritual aspects, if any, of your relationship. Faith is often cleaved to in times of hardship, if you are a person of faith, where do you run to when the storms of life are knocking down your door? Does one of you run to Jesus and the other to Buddha? Does one of you have absolutely no belief in God at all? If ever you have children, which god will your child serve?

There is a program we watched once called *Pregnant In Heels* in which one episode showed a rich couple who had an inter-faith marriage. The wife was a Christian and the husband was a Jew. They knew that trying to incorporate the values of their different faiths into their wedding day would be tricky, so they decided that a non-religious wedding ceremony would be less hassle all around. They forgot, however, to consider what impact their different faiths would have when adding children to the equation. The couple were in dispute, as the wife wanted her unborn daughter to become a Christian and to take part in all the traditions pertaining to Christianity, while the husband was set on an upbringing based primarily upon Jewish customs. As they were unable to resolve the issue, they hired a mediator to shed some light on the topic. When the mediator dug deeper, their reasoning's for wanting their child to be brought up in a specific way was not deeply rooted in the core beliefs of their individual faith, but was simply about wanting the child growing up in the way that they did. Because of this realisation, they were able to work things out, but what would have happened if they were really both steadfast in their religious beliefs?

Similarly, when visiting a friend who had just given birth in hospital, we noticed a Christian lady who had just given birth to a premature baby for a man who practices Islam, having a heated discussion on the ward. The man wanted to ensure that his son had a Muslim name and the lady was dead set against it. This issue was causing arguments on the hospital ward while the baby slept none the wiser in the transparent neo-natal cot. With all the stress of having to deal with the unexpected early birth of a baby, had they believed in the same God from the start, this problem may not have arisen.

At the same time however, we would like to be clear that even though you may start believing in the same source, as people grow and change, this does not always ensure that these beliefs will last a lifetime. Sadly, one married couple we have counselled, are on the verge of separation, simply because, although their choice to marry was primarily based upon the mutual beliefs of their faith, the wife woke up one day and simply decided she no longer holds these beliefs. She changed as a person and they are finding it hard to hold onto their once so sacred love. It is still possible to work through these differences, however, it depends on how much value is placed on the relationship by the two people involved in relation to the importance of their beliefs.

As a unit, Selone and I both love Jesus and have gone through some very difficult times in our marriage due to the cards that life sometimes deals. However, through our commitment to each other, and the word of God, we were able to hold one another up with scriptures in times of weakness, and see the light at the end of the tunnel. We are not saying it is impossible to have a relationship when two people have different faiths, but when life throws its curve balls, it is often easier if you cleave to the same source. Therefore, investing in ensuring you have spiritual unity is not something one should overlook.

Time and commitment, managing emotional baggage and working to ensure spiritual harmony are all attributes worth investing in if you want your relationship to flourish as you walk through the Yellow or courtship stage.

Take a moment to consider the level of investment being made into your current joint piggy bank or what adjustments you may have to make when you enter into a new relationship. Note down any thoughts here:

Chapter Nine

COMMON COURTESY

Taking the common courtesy to think about your significant other and your relationship in relation to the people around you during the Yellow stage will aid the likelihood of all relationships lasting and flourishing. Key points to consider are:

- Balancing your time with your partner, friends, family, and also pursuing your dreams and aspirations.

- Setting and managing expectations for your relationship.

- Showing respect and care for one another.

- Keeping up appearances.

Let's kick-start with balance. You need to make every attempt to ensure that the scales of life and your relationship balance as much as possible. By this, we mean taking time out to consider whether you have been missing-in-action from your close friends and family, simply because you are now crazy in love with your new partner. In most cases, real friends have been there for you before the beginning of time, and may have even been around before your romantic relationship began. They will hopefully still be around whether your relationship comes to a grinding halt, or if you ask them to collect the dress and hat for your special day that they put on lay away so many years before. The probability of this, however, depends on how well you balance your scales. We hear it all the time, best friends feeling let down by the fact that their needs are no longer being met. Instead, their friend's focus has shifted entirely, to maintaining their new romantic relationship with their partner. In the same way, being dedicated to a fault to your Yellow stage love, could mean you also begin to neglect the purpose you were designed for. If you find yourself too loved up to pursue your goals and dreams, unable to meet everyday obligations and suddenly unreliable to everyone else other than your partner, you may need to check your scales.

Now balance isn't in the interests of everyone, especially a possessive Yellow stage mate. If the imbalance in your life favours their side of the scale whereby they have you all to themselves and wish to keep it that way, they may show some resistance to you seeking to restore equilibrium. A good Yellow stage love is selfless enough to desire for you to have balance, a bad Yellow stage love will do everything in their power, even in subtle and seemingly loving ways to prevent this from happening. This can be a serious Red Flag as to whether moving forward in a relationship of this kind is a good idea. As human beings, we need interactions with various sources and people to thrive and maximise our potential. If there is someone in your life trying to prevent you from achieving this, something is terribly wrong. If you don't have balance in your relationships, important people and pressing things that need attention to attain your goals and dreams don't tend to wait around. You need to be aware and prepared to lose almost everything you love if you decide to leave this area unchecked.

If you are in a relationship, consider asking those closest to you (or just thinking about it objectively) if they feel you have the right balance. If you are not in a relationship, this is an opportunity to explore how well you are balancing your time, without a partner. This may give you insight on where you will need to improve once you begin a relationship. Be prepared; however, to self reflect deeply and honestly, especially if you don't get the response you desire. Note down what you have learnt here:

My goals and dreams are:

1. ....

2. ....

3. ....

If you are in a romantic relationship, how well are you doing at pursuing your goals and dreams? Do you feel your partner is: *(Please tick one option)*

1. Encouraging you to pursue your goals and dreams ☐

2. Keeping you from achieving your goals and dreams ☐

3. Indifferent about you achieving your goals and dreams ☐

4. Not even aware of what your goals and dreams are ☐

How focused on your dreams are you: *(Please tick one option)*

1. Very focused ☐

2. Fairly focused ☐

3. Not focused at all ☐

Why have you chosen the responses you have?

Would you like this to change so you can maintain: friendships, relationships with family members, or pursuing each other's goals and dreams? *(Please tick one option)*

1. Yes ☐

2. No ☐

3. N/A ☐

Three things I can do to improve the balance in my life are:

1. ....

2. ....

3. ....

Another issue that often causes trouble when we talk about common courtesy is negating to set and then manage expectations within a relationship.

Some people expect their partner to call them at least seven times a day, while at work with their micro-managing boss hovering over their shoulder. Others expect to be taken out on a date five days a week, everyday after work, always at 5:45pm. Some expect for the lady to always pay for the meal and for the man to always organise and pay for the Addison Lee taxi. By the time they get to the phrase "But that's not what I was expecting!" it often means that all of these important aspects have been overlooked and that they need to go back to square one, detailing their expectations of each other within the relationship, making sure they are realistic and also mutual. Ninety percent of all disappointments stem from unrealistic expectations. So taking the time out to make sure they are realistic in the first place can save you a lot of unnecessary drama.

Seeking to manage expectations aligns with showing respect and care for your mate. This is a very important aspect in helping a person to feel treasured and loved. It can be as simple as waiting up to ensure they got home safely, removing Facebook pictures of you with your ex partner, making a point not to make comparisons between them and previous partners, talking to them in a way that builds them up rather than tears them down, and finally, never doing anything that would forever cloud the relationship with doubt. For those of you that are directly or indirectly allowing yourself to be treated with anything but the utmost respect, we urge you to stop and think. No matter how you feel about a person, self-respect should always be at the top of your agenda. People can only treat you in the way you show them how. In the same way, do onto others, as you would have them do onto you.

Whether you are in a relationship or not, name three basic things you would expect from your partner:

1. ....

2. ....

3. ....

Consider the following:

Are these exceptions reasonable?

Yes ☐

No ☐

Is your partner aware of them?

Yes ☐

No ☐

Have you discussed how possible it is to meet them?

Yes ☐

No ☐

Are both parties happy to adhere to them?

Yes ☐

No ☐

How could you lovingly command more respect in your relationship?

1. ....

2. ....

3. ....

How could you show more respect?

1. ....

2. ....

3. ....

Showing respect and care for your partner is a very good practice, but showing respect and care for yourself is even more valuable. How well do you look after your mind, soul, and body? If you don't regularly tune yourself up and keep on top of all the things you need to do, to allow you to function well as a person, you may indeed be heading for a break down. Simple things that keep you healthy and being your best inside and out are:

- Healthy diet

- Exercise

- Taking short regular breaks (e.g. Spas or nature walks)

- Spending time by yourself

Taking care of yourself, by at least trying to keep up appearances, is also common courtesy towards your partner. We don't mean keeping up appearances in the sense that you are just painting a façade of who you are, we simply mean being mindful of how you present yourself to the world and your partner. Even though physical attraction is not the most important thing in a relationship, let's face it, it is definitely a factor, and it can help to enliven or maintain a spark in the relationship. Is that beer belly and those extra few rolls in the waistline a feature that was present when you first met? If not is it something that either of you mind? If it is starting to get in the way, take action and do something about it supporting each other the whole way to the gym! Don't get us wrong, we are not glamorous twenty-four seven, and those of you who have seen the *At Home With The Ajewole's* video will be able to attest to that! Even so, we make a point to remain in shape and stay healthy, for aesthetically pleasing reasons yes, but more so to increase the likelihood of a longer and healthier life together. This extends also to your mental health. Maintaining a peaceful state as far as possible will result in more peaceful interaction and a much healthier relationship overall.

What three things can you do to keep up appearances?

1. ....

2. ....

3. ....

So, common courtesy therefore needs to be applied to ensure balance, realistic expectations, respect, care and keeping up appearances are all in place. Taking the time to make yourselves aware of these issues and then taking the appropriate action to improve them in consideration of yourself and your partner will most definitely aid a happy and joyous Yellow stage.

Chapter Ten

CULTURE SHOCK

Unlike in the past, interracial relationships are more widely accepted and are very common in many parts of the world, especially in the United Kingdom. Don't get us wrong, some people still, whether in public or private can't stand the thought of someone of one race falling in love with and procreating with someone of a different race. Deeper still, some people have an issue with people of the same race being together if they are from different countries or even from different regions within the same country! G and I fall into one of these categories. We are both Black, but his family are from West Africa and mine are from the Caribbean. If we trace our ancestry back a few generations it is highly likely that my Caribbean roots began somewhere in West Africa. Nevertheless, in both our cultures we are seen as vastly different. These differences were never an issue for us, but it was for a small segment of so-called friends and family who would make distasteful and derogatory 'jokes' about each other's Caribbean or African heritage. Traditionally speaking, G being from the Yoruba tribe in Nigeria meant that he was destined to marry a Yoruba lady or at least someone from another part of Nigeria. By choosing a St Lucian queen to be his bride, he had gone against everything his culture and tradition advocate for. Thankfully, both of our mothers had more of a liberal approach to tradition and culture and had fallen in love with each of us as people and wanted nothing else but for us to be happy together. We had to decide therefore whether worrying about other people's opinions would add any cubits to our height. Since it wouldn't, we decided not to give a second thought to what anyone else had to say!

Similarly, a major, recurring issue that arises within the relationship counselling we conduct surrounds issues of perception a person's family has with the person they have chosen, rather than actual experiences that have occurred specifically between them. In most cases, this concern is not about the person's partner being a bad influence, who would lead their loved one astray, but rather about them simply being the wrong type of person because they are from a different culture, the wrong culture! If even those closest to us (such as our mothers) had raised these types of concerns we would have asked ourselves the following questions and would advise couples experiencing something similar to do the same thing:

- How important to me, are the people who are concerned about who I have chosen as my mate?

- Are the people who have these concerns about my chosen mate part of the majority or minority of people in my life?

- If it's the majority, can they still be wrong?

- Does their concern come from a good place? Do they have the right motives?

- Even so, do they have a good basis for their argument, as in are they unhappy with the way my mate is treating me or does it stem from underlying prejudices surrounding tradition and culture?

- If I were to go against their advice, would they still continue being a part of my life?

- If they were prepared to sever all ties with me if I continue a relationship with this person, how much would this affect me?

- If they do decide to dissolve our friendship/relationship based on my defiance, was it ever real in the first place?

- Have I had a real heart to heart about this with myself?

- Have my partner and I discussed the issues we are facing regarding this?

- Have I sought spiritual counsel through prayer or meeting with my Pastor or someone with strong Christian faith?

- Do I really know much about the culture of my partner and his community?

- Am I clear that embracing a new culture that is different from my own may be a difficult thing to do, especially in ones that outwardly expresses themselves such as a particular way of dressing (e.g.

individuals from the Yoruba tribe in Nigeria typically wear traditional attires and head-wraps to special events)?

- Is my mate supportive enough to clearly explain all these different practices that are custom to them, while alien to me? Would they be happy for me to decline to partake in certain parts of it if I so wish?

- Am I happy to regularly visit the country of my spouse and or even set up home there in the future and raise a family with these values in mind?

- Do I ultimately realise that only I can live my life?

By coaching couples with various issues, including those, which pertain to different cultures and customs, we have found that someone on the outside looking in will always have an opinion, and it is ultimately impossible to even try to please everyone. There is nothing we haven't heard, "He's too fat, too thin, too dark, too light!" the list is endless! What matters most is the two of you, and how hard you are willing to work together to learn about each other's cultures, and whether or not you are flexible enough to compromise on any aspects that make the other party uncomfortable.

For example, during my pregnancy with our first son, G and I talked long and hard about one aspect of his culture pertaining to the birth of a new baby. In my culture, or at least within my extended family, not much fuss is typically made over a new life entering the world. In stark contrast, however, Yorubas see this as such a special occasion that needs to be marked and celebrated. Traditional Yoruba naming ceremonies usually occur on the eighth day after the birth of a child, where the names of the child are revealed to close family and friends, and there is a spiritual celebration to honour this. We had been to several ceremonies during our Yellow stage so I had a fair idea of what it would entail. Even so, this was not something I had been used to in my culture.

I contemplated on whether or not I would be able to manage it a mere eight days after becoming a mother for the first time. G reminded me of how important it was to him and for his family stating that I would not need to lift a finger, reassuring me that the hype would calm down after about three weeks and no one would even remember we existed. In addition he highlighted that our son would be showered with prayers, gifts and love. When I thought about it in that way and could see how important it was to him; I agreed to go ahead. Embracing something so different and on such a grand scale was daunting, but also liberating.

We did not include every aspect of the traditional ceremony, just those we both felt comfortable with. All relationships are about giving and taking and by agreeing to marry someone from a different culture, I have agreed to at least try to be involved with some things that he holds dear, and G does the same for me.

It is advisable that present cultural issues, and issues that could arise in the foreseeable future are addressed during the Yellow stage, way before thoughts of marriage are floating around in the air. Many wars have begun over the rules of tradition and culture and the way that *things have always been done*. You can avoid these wars in your own home by contemplating on the points mentioned earlier. We are not advocating for a rebellion of culture and tradition, and the extinction of all those who try hard to preserve it, but rather, some proactive thinking of the value you both wish to place on it in your lives together.

If you are in a relationship, list some of the cultural issues you and your mate have faced or envision facing in the future:

1. ....

2. ....

3. ....

How did you or do you plan to overcome them?

1. ....

2. ....

3. ....

If you are not in a relationship, how open will you be to embracing traditions from another culture? *(Please tick one option)*

1. Totally willing ☐

2. Mostly willing ☐

3. Partially willing ☐

4. Not at all willing ☐

Are there any particular issues or traditions (within you or your partner's culture) that you would not be willing to compromise on?

Based on your responses, how important is it that the partner you choose is from the same culture as you? *(Please tick one option)*

1. Totally important ☐

2. Partially important ☐

3. Not at all important ☐

"Therefore a man leaves his father and mother and embraces his wife. They become one flesh." (Genesis 2:24 MSG)

Is it time for you to cut mummy's apron strings? Only you can decide…

Chapter Eleven

CAN YOU WAIT?

Even though everyone else seems to be doing it, as Christians, we believe that God created sex as an expression of love for **married couples only**! Being that the society we live in now advocates differently may mean that this concept is a very hard pill to swallow and possibly not one you are interested in hearing about. After all, reading any further may cause you to question your current attitude to sex and make you uncomfortable enough for you to consider looking at things in a different way. Even though this is likely to be an unpopular concept with many and irrespective of your previous sexual exploits, from here on out, we are bold enough to ask you the question: **"Can you wait?"**

We believe waiting until you are married to either have sex for the first time or to continue having sex is a good idea. It would be beneficial for us all to adhere to as individuals and as a society for a number of profound reasons we are about to explore.

First of all, sex should be seen as sacred and respected above all else. British society sets the age of consent at sixteen, but at sixteen, are we really ready to handle everything that comes along with sexual intimacy? It is so much more than just a physical act and therefore when it is undertaken outside of its original design, with the wrong person and at the wrong time it can have dire consequences. From working in Pastoral Care in education, I have had to counsel countless number of girls who regretted having sex for the first time in their school uniform, with the popular guy, behind the bike shed. Even if the effects of this do not seem to be immediately or directly manifested in the here and now, it can catch up with you later on.

People that indulge in sexual activity outside of marriage have given a piece of themselves that they can never ever get back. Whether you are aware of it or not, this can have a negative impact on any future relationships, especially in the partnership with the person that you believe to be 'The One'. Sometimes the consequences of participating in the physical act of having sex with someone we are not married to can extend beyond the moments of sexual intercourse. We know people who have intended to simply have a one or two night stand with someone and have subsequently and (not intentionally in most cases) put themselves in the position of carrying a child and having to co-parent or single parent for a person who's middle name or favourite colour is still a mystery. In an instant, the direction that their life was heading in has totally shifted. Based on the circumstances in which this child has been conceived, they are then faced with the dilemma of either continuing with the pregnancy or deciding to abort an innocent child (that so many women do not have the privilege of experiencing), just because of the situation by which the pregnancy had come about. If these two individuals were married to the person God intended for them, this would not have been an issue they would ever have to be faced with. "But what if it wasn't a one night stand and you fell pregnant by your partner who you have been with for seven years within the confines of a loving relationship? Surely that makes it a bit better because you are practically married anyway!" we hear you wonder. Better maybe, but still not ideal in the way God created it, because practically married is still unfortunately, not married. From being both parents now and a husband and wife first, it is unclear to us why some people would want to, or not take precautions to avoid taking on the responsibility of raising a child over that of being someone's life partner. In other words, having a child is not seen as such a big deal in the same way that marriage is. For us, being parents is much more challenging than just being husband and wife. However, taking on this responsibility as husband and wife has made the process much easier, as we are both equally able to share the load of parenting, and have already been bold enough to commit to each other indefinitely. This gives us a sense of security within marriage and child rearing, that we may not otherwise have. Now, we know that divorce does happen, but because a marriage is legally binding, and courtship or cohabitation is not, it is much harder to walk away.

Similarly, it's advisable to wait until you are married to live with your partner. We did, and believe all couples should, as helps to minimise the temptation to have sex before marriage, and it gives you the complete, new experience of becoming husband and wife. It also minimises the chances of somebody not wanting to buy the cow as they are getting the milk for free. Sociologist Neil Bennett (1988) reported that eighty percent of cohabiting women were more likely to separate or divorce than those who did not live with their husbands before marriage. If we don't act like we are married before we are actually married, this will hopefully not be our fate.

Other reasons why we believe waiting to have sex is a good idea is because, if every single person in the world would have waited until they married one person to engage in sexual activity, the likelihood of sexually transmitted diseases and HIV/Aids related deaths would have been significantly reduced. There would be no prostitution, no people mistaking sex for love and no guys bantering in the pub with derogatory phrases like "I had her and she was better than her friend, you should give it a go!"

In today's society where sex is everywhere and abstinence is hiding somewhere behind a rock in the desert, a new vow of celibacy until marriage to the right person is possible and can have the following benefits:

- The risk of contracting a sexually transmitted disease is decreased.

- There is a lower risk of an unwanted pregnancy.

- There is a newness and a powerful connection on your wedding night and throughout your married life.

- You can make love to the person you are one hundred percent committed to in complete freedom.

- You can learn together how to improve your sessions of intimacy.

- The value placed on making love is much higher than it would be with a random guy or girl.

- You can have awkward moments during intimacy and just laugh about it because you are free!

Guys and girls, if you are already in a relationship where having sex with each other is common place, a new vow of celibacy will only work if both parties:

- Buy into the concept wholeheartedly.

- Are willing to think more long term than short term.

- Intend to marry each other in the near future for reasons other than just sex.

- Are ready to change some of previously common practices (such as undressing in front of each other).

- Value each other enough to wait.

If you are yet to get into a new relationship, the person you choose will need to understand and support all of the above and place greater value upon you than their need for immediate sexual satisfaction. Perhaps you would need to make this clear in the Red stage so not to disappoint your mate should you move into the Yellow stage where they may be shocked to find that the *sweetie shop* is not open for business until the Green stage. Their understanding and agreement would be paramount to a successful relationship.

We watched a reality show a few years ago with Terry Cruz and his family where his daughter was about twelve years old and she was all dressed up in an evening gown at a Purity Ball event with her dad. She along with a host of other young girls took a vow of purity until marriage symbolised by the wearing of a ring and sealed by a dance with her father. The thing that stood out the most was when the vow included the line: "**I will not give a boyfriend husband privileges**" and when you do give your body before you have the wedding ring, that is exactly what you're doing. A lot of cultures and religions also still try to uphold this moral standing in a world that has become so liberal in recent years. If you feel ready, how about taking a new vow of celibacy?

Celibacy Vow (Repeat aloud)

"The treasure in my treasure box, from this day forth I will keep locked, to open only when I see, the love they have is just for me. I wont give away the key, to someone not on bended knee, holding tight that special thing, for that night they give the wedding ring"

Celibacy thoughts:

I see the value of taking a new vow of celibacy and want to wait until I am married to have sex because:

My concerns around undertaking this challenge now pertain to:

Even though I am committed to achieving the goal, I believe it will be **easy/hard** *(Please circle correct response)* to stick to it because:

Someone who will not judge me and I can be accountable to is:

If you don't have someone you can be accountable to without judgement, you may need to garner extra strength and be accountable to yourself.

I will try my utmost to adhere to it but if I fall I will *(Please tick one option)*:

1. Acknowledge what I have done, dust my self off and report it to a trusted person/myself and continue on with my vow ☐

Or:

2. Revert backwards, renouncing my vow in its entirety ☐

I believe my mate will (*Please tick all that apply*):

1. Be supportive and participate ☐
2. Be unsupportive and pull away ☐
3. Wonder if I have gone crazy and try to change my mind ☐
4. Potentially leave me (if they do, you need to question whether it was true love in the first place) ☐
5. Potentially seek to satisfy their needs elsewhere (if they do, this is more about them than it has ever been about you) ☐
6. Five things I can do to aid a new vow of celibacy are (*e.g. avoiding the type of people I normally attract or considering making like minded friends etc):*

1. ....

2. ....

3. ....

4. ....

5. ....

I feel ready to undertake this **now/in the future** (*Please circle correct response*)

I have/am going to approach my friend _____ to see if they may be willing to undertake this challenge with me

If you choose to have sex outside of marriage, just remember, a moment of passion can lead to a lifetime of pain…

Can you wait? We know it's a big task but we hope and believe that you can.

Chapter Twelve

"I DO"... BUT DO YOU REALLY?

On numerous occasions, I have had to sign contractual agreements, from a monthly payment plan on a phone to a mortgage agreement with the bank. Before signing on the doted line, it was advisable for me to look through what I was signing myself up for, and to make sure the contract was agreeable by both parties. It is always surprising to witness how many people then, caught in the euphoria and the ecstasy of getting engaged, negate the very important question of **"What am I getting myself into?"** No matter how good of an offer the mortgage lenders or the telephone company put on the table, it is worthwhile reading the small print, to ensure the offer is really as good as it sounds. The same goes for couples who are considering becoming engaged. This is the time to ensure the right inventories are taken to eliminate any 'unwelcome surprises' in the future.

Way too many people say "I do", without actually realising that they are about to sign a lifetime contractual agreement that will have a huge impact on their own life, their partner's life, and the lives of their children and extended families. Before walking down the aisle, before booking the Church and the flowers, before putting the deposit on the flat, before sending out the beautifully handcrafted invitations, before booking your dream honeymoon to the Maldives, and the all important John Lewis or Argos gift list, it is vital that there is a period of time when sanity is restored, and the soon to be engaged couple take a reality check on what they are getting into. Marriage is beautiful, but is also serious business!

If and when a married couple run into trouble, they will often try to get the necessary help and support needed to mend any broken links in their relationship. However, one of the things that many people neglect is getting the right support, and asking those difficult questions before they actually get married. It is extremely important, even paramount, for a couple to sit down together, and also within the setting of a professional or faith-based Counsellor before entering into marriage. It is at this stage that issues need to be ironed out regarding how the couple plans to design and map out their lives together. It is at this stage that the loved up and excited couple needs to ask themselves what their expectations of life will be like after those two life changing words "I do" are uttered, after the groom has kissed the bride at the altar, after they've checked out of the honeymoon suite, and after all the wedding guests have returned back to Scunthorpe and Liverpool.

Having set and agreed expectations of marriage, children, roles within the home, finances, annual holidays, church, and much more, it makes life for the newlyweds a lot more enjoyable, and avoids anyone being blamed for false advertising. It was important for us to sit together, with trusted spiritual counsel (a few months before our wedding day) over a cup of hot chocolate, and set a lifelong vision for ourselves and our future children, that would ensure we enter into our lifelong commitment to each other, with both our eyes wide open.

Some couples don't talk about how many children they want, if any before they get married. Others fail to talk about if an annual holiday is a necessity or a luxury, who will be responsible for disciplining the children, who will take out the bins, if one or both desire to pursue further education once married, which Church will they attend etc. Good Pre-marital counselling or Pre-marriage coaching helps a couple to see the bigger picture, and address issues that are often left untouched because of the sensitivity of the issues or even more alarming, because of the stress of planning the 'Big Day!'

Pre-marital counselling focuses on the realities of marriage, and how each person will overcome these challenges. In this respect, pre-marital counselling deals with much the same areas as marriage counselling, but from a different perspective. Instead of a retrospective approach examining how a problem developed, an anticipatory perspective is taken. A prospective husband or wife needs to become aware of what difficulties they will face and how they are likely to respond. There are issues that all married people will face, and other challenges that may result from the unique characteristics of each individual involved, and their particular experiences and circumstances.

Whenever we conduct pre-marital counselling sessions for couples, we have approximately sixty questions that we walk the couples through, which can take up to six one-hour sessions. Usually, half of the questions and issues have never crossed the minds of those about to be married. Good pre-marital counselling will prepare you properly for the road ahead.

Preparing for your life long commitment to each other before marriage will help alleviate some of the unnecessary stress and feelings of disappointment many couples face after their wedding day. It will also help set you up for a successful financial, emotional, sexual, spiritual future as a married couple. Additionally, research has shown that pre-marital counselling reduces the likelihood of divorce by thirty percent. Divorce can turn your whole world upside down, so any steps you can take before marriage to avoid it is a good idea indeed. While pre-marital counselling and stopping to ask yourself those all important questions before saying "I do" can't guarantee you won't encounter storms and curveballs in your marriage, the training in communication and conflict resolution and the discussion of expectations, compatibility, intimacy, goals, and finances will definitely help you deal with some of the main strains that can arise in a marriage.

Yes, you are madly in love and eager to live happily ever after, but before saying "I do", it is worthwhile sitting down to discuss how compatible you truly are. This is not a compatibility test to see if you love each other or are right for each other. Our sincere hope is that you already know you are by this stage. However, it is important to know that irrespective of how much you are besotted with each other, you're likely to have different habits, different approaches to handling finances, different expectations when it comes to intimacy, differences in your family background, differences in your fears and anxiety of married life, often but not totally shaped by your own family history of relationships. Either way, there are a number of things you need to think about before making a lifetime commitment. The answers to these questions may help you decide what will keep your marriage afloat when so many others are sinking.

Things to consider before saying "I do"

Solid foundations:

- If all was stripped away, are we good friends?

Sharing:

- Would we give each other our last Rolo?

Gender roles:

- Can he/she cook and clean? Would they be willing to learn? Would the division of household duties be equal?

- What if only the female worked, would the man be expected to run the home? Would the woman be expected to help?

Spirituality:

- Do we worship the same God? Will it cause conflict later on if we don't?

- How much implication has our faith (if at all) had on our decision to get married?

Finances:

- Does she have a fetish for Jimmy Choo shoes?

- Would he/she still value me if I could no longer provide the type of lifestyle he/she had become accustomed to?

- What's my future spouses attitude to credit? Does he/she have outstanding debt? Am I happy to take this on once we become one?

- Is he/she going overboard with spending for the wedding day? Would they listen if I asked them to stop?

Sacrifice:

- What do I have to give up to be with him/her? Am I willing to? Is it worth it?

Family planning:

- Does he/she like or want children? Do I?

- Do we have similar parental styles? Am I quick to smack, and him/her to laugh it off?

- If there are children from a previous marriage/relationship what arrangements have been made for custody, financial support and visitation? How comfortable am I with the arrangements?

Extended family:

- Will we live near to our extended family? Do we want to? Does it matter now? Will it matter if we have children?

- Do we get on with each other's family? Does this matter to us?

- Are our families in total support of our intention to marry? Does it matter to us?

Boundaries:

- Will we put boundaries in place to safeguard our marriage (including for those nosy, interfering mother in laws)?

- Are there any external relationships my partner has with the opposite sex that I am not comfortable continuing when we get married?

Loyalty and commitment:

- Would my future spouse do whatever they had to for our family to survive?

- Would I be willing to support my spouse come what may?

Conflict resolution:

- Do we resolve conflict well? If not, are we working on it?

Life's curveballs

- Can we handle the uncertainties of life together?

- Are we built on something authentic enough to outlast the storms that life could potentially throw at us?

Love and passion:

- Are we in love and do we work on making sure this flourishes?

- Is he/she still attractive to me? Am I? Do we do our best to ensure we are?

- Are there any sexual habits, fantasises or preferences that either of us are likely to be uncomfortable with?

Caring:

- If I were sick, would he/she nurse me back to health? Would I be willing do the same for my spouse irrespective of the extra responsibility I may have to assume?

Expectations of a husband/wife:

- Is my future spouse aware of my expectations of them? Are they realistic?

Soul searching:

- Is there anything that makes me jealous of my fiancé?

- What changes do I plan to make in my life to benefit our relationship?

- Do I realise that current relationships with family or friends may change? Am I truly prepared for this?

- What is my greatest fear as I think about the prospect of a future marriage or as I approach marriage? How can this fear be overcome?

- Is there anyone else I would rather spend the rest of my life with?

- Do I view marriage as permanent?

- **Is divorce an option for either of us?**

As you may have noticed, a lot of the points you need to consider before saying "I do" are aspects touched upon earlier within the Yellow stage. This lends support to the notion that you need to have the Yellow stage properly in order before you can even dream about moving onto a fruitful Green stage. If the responses to these questions are more negative than positive, you need to discuss whether moving forward at this point is a good idea. If it doesn't seem salvageable or both parties are not willing to make changes to improve things before the question is popped, you may have to be strong enough to let it go and move onto brighter days either by yourself, or in time, with someone new.

The reason the last bullet point is written in bold is because a 20 year old male divorcee sat in tears in our office because although divorce wasn't an option for him, it was for his newly titled ex-wife. From the very beginning, make sure that divorce is not an option, for either of you.

Marriage to the right person is such a beautiful thing; to the wrong person it could be hell on earth. Because this is for life, you need to choose your spouse very wisely. If somebody told a certain celebrity couple this information in advance, perhaps their marriage would have lasted longer than a mere seventy-two days.

> ### *If you never make divorce an option,*
> ### *there are certain things you will never say or do.*

Ready for the Green and ultimate stage? Lets go!

Stage 3

GREEN (MARRIAGE)

The Green stage in *The Colours of Love* paradigm symbolises a state of harmony and fulfilment within marriage. Irrespective of what life throws at you, we believe that this type of serenity should be already founded and then built upon in a marriage. The Green stage therefore is the pinnacle place where all Red and Yellow stage participants should strive to not only attain, but also more importantly, maintain. There is some overlap when discussing engagement, as a couple is effectively in transition between the Yellow and Green stage. We have chosen to address this within the Green stage, as the couple are en route to marriage.

The majority of the time, marriage should be a tranquil and safe place where the person you have chosen to spend the rest of your days on earth with is simply everything you could ever need in a mate. In order to achieve this almost constant state of bliss, like in all the other stages, there are certain concepts you need to be aware of and work diligently upon. These include:

- Understanding what marriage is.

- Whilst engaged ensuring you focus more on the 'Big Life' rather than just the 'Big Day.'

- How to make both life and wedding day plans.

- Understanding that ninety-nine percent of marriage is everyday life.

- Expressions of love.

- Protecting your family.

- Knowing how to preserve the freshness.

- Managing finances.

- Handling life's curveballs.

- Checking in on each other in terms of how the relationship is going.

Whether you are in a Green stage, striving for it or fighting to maintain it, being conscious and responsive to these ideas can help you create and maintain a safe haven for you, your partner and your family for life.

MARRIAGE DEFINED

To most people, a happy marriage is the pinnacle or the holy grail of all successful relationships. Various cultures across the world have varying definitions of what marriage is. Usually, marriage is defined as an institution in which interpersonal relationships, typically sexual and intimate, are acknowledged. Further, *'Marriage is a relationship in which two people have **pledged** themselves to **each other for life** in the manner of husband and wife that is recognised legally, religiously or socially, granting the participants mutual conjugal **rights and responsibilities**.'* From the bolded section you can see that in a marriage there are rights but there are also responsibilities, which have to be fulfilled in order for the marriage to flourish and survive *indefinitely.*

Many cultures limit marriage between two people of opposite genders, while some cultures permit same-sex marriages and recognise marriage to multiple partners, this is often known as polygamy. As Christians we believe that marriage is God's great idea between one man and one woman. We were created to be social beings, to live in relationship and to build communities. Under the umbrella of marriage, if we nurture it, we are able to enjoy a fulfilling and exciting life.

Chapter Thirteen

THE BIG DAY VS THE BIG LIFE

"Wedding favours? Check. Champagne glasses? Check. Horse and carriage? Check. £6,000 pound wedding dress? Double check! Sexy lingerie? Check! White chocolate fountain? Check. Hair and make up? Check. Banging DJ? Check!! Real and well thought out life plans? Unchecked"

Sound familiar? Well, it does to us. We get it, for a lot of people, making your big day as big and memorable as possible is at the forefront of your mind. With all this excitement however, we beseech you, please consider this:

For your Green stage to be successful, you need to start off on the right foot. Just before you enter the Green stage and are officially engaged you should be more intentional about planning your life together rather than the small details of a twelve-hour day.

Wedding days are traditionally supposed to be one of the happiest days of your life. However, in reality, it can be one of the most stressful and draining days that become a distant memory in your minds if you so much as blink during the ceremony. Remember, the core of your wedding day is simply a public declaration between God and man (or just man) that you love and intend to commit to this special person for the rest of the time you have here together on earth. Everything else apart from that is simply extra. Extra that you can do without, extra that you could end up paying for five years after you have been married, extra that the people you love may just slate and put down anyway, extra to the point where you struggle to eat or pay the rent or mortgage during your married life, extra to the extreme where you forfeit a honeymoon to the Bahamas just so your guests can have the *platinum* rather than *bronze* wedding package! Jokes aside, there is a true cost for extras! Don't let all of these unnecessary things cloud your judgment about what's really important.

What is actually important is 'The Big Life' rather than 'The Big Day'. When we were getting married, we were more excited about being husband and wife and living day to day as this rather than the wedding day itself. Towards the end of our planning period, we simply wanted to get the formalities of the day out of the way! Deciding to place more emphasis on the planning of our lives together as we transitioned from the Yellow to the Green stage, meant that it did not matter how the weather was (it rained by the way) or whether the fried rice would be authentic enough. These things did not dictate how we felt about each other; we chose not to let these issues influence the very serious commitment we were about to make. Taking this stance meant that we were pleasantly surprised on the day and were able to pause long enough to take in the breath taking scenery of Richmond Park and we enjoyed it way more than we ever thought we would.

So in terms of making plans, believe it or not, we began making wedding and future life plans well before hubby even popped the question. Because of the plans we had already made together and being clear on the direction we wanted to head in, it became easy for me to accept his proposal. We knew that making good, well thought out plans for the wedding day was important, but making plans for our lives together was even more important. In this chapter we will discuss exactly how we did both.

The Big Life: Life Plans

G was ready to get married a lot sooner than I was. He would talk about it quite a bit during my first year of university. At that stage in my life, marriage was something that I saw way in my future and I didn't feel that I could manage the responsibility of it well enough at age nineteen while taking the 18 bus to university. By the time we were six years in, we had a real sense of who we were as individuals, who we were together and who we hoped to become, I started to feel a little more ready. During this period, we had been making plans of what we expected to have accomplished together within the next five years for instance. In order for any of these things to be even remotely possible, we realised that a concrete commitment to each other and our love would be a significant step to achieving all we desired. Moreover, G calmed my fears of becoming a wife by uttering these few simple words: **"Life is just a journey and I just want to go on that journey with you"** Once the last syllable left his lips, he had me; I was sold! The idea of marriage no longer felt scary, distant or complicated. He said so much in so little words and appeased all my concerns about the expectations of a wife or life partner. The fact he depicted it as a 'journey', meant to me that the road may not be smooth, and although there might be ups and downs, you press along towards your goal, together. From here onwards I was ready to be his wife.

Knowing for certain that we were ready, and more so willing to commit to each other indefinitely, made the life planning process a lot easier. It simply involved regular and intentional conversations about what we desired for our future together. At times, topics were as simple as what colour scheme we would like for the flat, or how we are going to split the chores, to whether or not we want children, when to have them, and how we aim to grow together spiritually. Having these short but sweet or sometimes intense and long conversations about the little things made the transition into being husband and wife fairly effortless. In retrospect however, we can see that maturity and new life experiences can put a shift in your focus, and subsequently affect future decisions so you must always be willing to change these plans for the good of your relationship. Once we had this area of our planning in order, we felt ready to move onto the actual wedding planning.

If you are in a relationship right now, answer the following questions. If you are not in a relationship now, you can answer these questions in terms of what you envision for your relationship or can just come back to this exercise when your relationship status changes.

What three goals or life plans do you have for yourself?

1. ....

2. ....

3. ....

What three goals or life plans does your partner have?

1. ....

2. ....

3. ....

What three goals or life plans do you have as a couple?

1. ....

2. ....

3. ....

Have you set aside adequate time and attention to explore the 'little things' pertaining to your future together?

Yes ☐

No (If no, please do) ☐

Are there any areas of disagreement about your future life plans that may cause contention later on?

Yes ☐

If yes, please list this below and discuss how you plan to overcome it:

No ☐

How do you envision 'The Big Life' to be?

How does your partner envision 'The Big Life' to be?

The Big Day: Wedding Plans

The Proposal

So he asked me the magic question on February 3rd 2007. I had spot cream on my face lounging around my mother's house with clashing house clothes and a multi-coloured headscarf. Predictable old G was supposed to ask me on the February 14th so as you can tell; I wasn't ready. He seemed really nervous, not like I had ever seen him before. It probably didn't help that I went into a fit of laughter once he accidently dropped the ring on my lap. Anyway, once I contained myself enough to speak and his nervous smile slowly faded away, I realised that this was serious, very serious, and it dawned on me just how much this little mummy's girl's life was about to change. As I said "Yes" we embraced and shed a tear and were now ready for the challenge that lay ahead. The next day, we cemented the in depth ideas we had already discussed about our wedding and drove to Richmond Park, fell in love with the manor house and booked it on the spot. Although we were devout followers of Christ, believe it or not, getting married in a church was not at the top of our list. We believe that God is present everywhere and we incorporated Him heavily during our blessing service at the manor house. It makes me chuckle when Christmas, weddings and funeral only church going Christians are adamant that they MUST have their wedding in a church. We got engaged in the February and were married in the September of the same year. If you have good project management and organisation and execution skills, planning can be done in seven months or less, just like it was for us. Having a wedding planner is not a pre-requisite to having a successful day, for us, it was just an extra cost that we could do without.

Equal Participation

We both participated equally in the planning process; it was a joint project where we visited wedding planning websites like www.confetti.co.uk, found their 'To Do List', and tailored it to make our own. At this point we realised that it was 'our' day, which we could arrange in any way we saw fit, and that traditional rules and regulations need not apply. For example, although I had a few close friends and cousins, I knew that given the timescale I didn't want to deal with all the headache of managing bridesmaids fittings where somebody doesn't like the style of dress chosen and wants to wear red rather than silver shoes! So, I simply asked my sister to be my Maid of Honour and her daughter to be our Flower Girl. In stark contrast,

G had about eight Groomsmen and a lot of stress might I add, with sorting out their attire! We basically worked from a few excel spreadsheets of tasks and communicated frequently over email, or on the phone, ensuring that the cake had been booked on time or that G had ordered the rings we tried on. We also made sure that we set reminder days to help us remember that the completion day for a specific task was fast approaching. It was basically us setting a deadline for our deadlines, which meant that one whole month before the wedding, all tasks and payments were complete and we were able to relax! During this time, to avoid 'wedding overkill' we also set aside one day each week where any talk of the wedding was absolutely forbidden. You should practice this also otherwise it can overtake everything to the point where you may forget to check in on each other and find out how the person you are about to marry is really doing.

Whether you are on the way to getting married, are married already or would like to be in the future, playing on each others strengths, and in the spirit of equal participation, which of these few wedding tasks would you give to yourself? Which would you hand to your partner and which would you do together?

Wedding Plans Task Division Table

Task	Me	Fiancé	Together
Booking the venue			
Organising the flowers			
Arranging the order of service			
Organising marriage licences			
Researching honeymoon destination			
Creating invitations			
Venue décor/colour scheme			
Arranging entertainment			
Financial budgeting			
Organising somewhere to live afterwards			
Organising the gift list			
Arranging transportation			

If one person believes that only they are capable of completing most of the tasks above, or only one person wants to willingly participate in the planning process, this is not a very good basis for the start of a life long union. It is a chance to learn and grow together and teach each other new skills.

Finances

Weddings and money, money and weddings, these two words go hand in hand! In terms of the financial side of things, I was blessed to have been given sound financial advice in regards to savings, while growing up. After contributing to my mother's household bills, I was able to save a large amount of money every month. We had to be prepared to see any extra financial support as a bonus, never factoring any pledges that were made with mere words. Most people wonder how much cash they would need to have their dream wedding, our thoughts surrounded how much we would need to have a nice, elegant, classic wedding, but still be able to eat after the wedding day and go an a nice honeymoon afterwards! This type of thinking made it easier to forgo certain seemingly necessary extras like the classic car. We were intending to spend the whole day in a manor house, why on earth would I need a classic car? My uncle's brand new BMW X5 with a bit of pink ribbon on the front was just fine for me while my hubby to be was driven in his friend's Range Rover Sport. In addition, we got married on a Monday. A Monday? Yes, a Monday, it was half the price for the venue hire when compared with a Saturday and minimised the chance of gatecrashers just 'being in the area'.

Saving well before hand and deciding to not spend another dime on the wedding a day after it was finished, meant that credit cards and loans were not an option. My older and more seasoned, married sister reminded us that we also needed to budget for at least the first month's set of bills afterwards. Financially, that really put into perspective what we could and couldn't afford to do. We understand that saving your own money and using that, to pay for your wedding rather than interest abundant credit, is a rather long option for most. However we had made a vow not to start our married life in debt, therefore for us, saving up was the only option. Perhaps you should consider adopting a similar train of thought and scaling back where possible. We know that not having the classic car, or other such items is not an option for some people, as they have the 'you only get married once' mentality, and want everything their heart desires. If for a moment you were able to consider the benefits of well thought out spending, what would you be prepared to do without?

Items we would be prepared to scale back on or forgo are:

1. ....

2. ....

3. ....

The Golden Ticket

When my friends and family learnt just how small of a wedding we were deciding to stage, they began jokingly calling their invitations "The Golden Ticket" denoting privilege and exclusivity in the most sarcastic manor possible. Looking back, it was true; we only wanted ninety special people who were truly 'for us' and what we stood for, to share our special day. Just to put this into context, we have been to weddings of people from our cultures that have had over a thousand people, where 'invite only' is a foreign concept and every man and his dog are permitted to partake in such an intimate moment. At the same time, we understand that some couples really do not want to leave anybody out. However unfortunately, sometimes this is more out of obligation, due to pressure from family, rather than a genuine desire for all these people to share in their special day. As you can see now, our wedding was very, very small in contrast. Having ninety guests brought about a real sense of reverence. During the speeches and sacred parts of the ceremony, you could hear a pin drop. That reverence is something I have never experienced in weddings that have a larger amount of guests in attendance. Despite some people being unhappy that they didn't get a 'Golden Ticket', the intimacy and respect from having such a small crowd made our decision worthwhile. You need to decide whether you want a 'Golden Ticket' or an 'All Welcome' type of affair.

Small Wedding Pros	Small Wedding Cons

Large Wedding Pros	Large Wedding Cons

Whether you choose to stage a grand wedding or a more intimate affair, when you enter the Green stage, one way to make a poignant connection between the big day and the big life is to create a **'Box of Vows'** where you each place inside a written copy of the legally binding, heartfelt vows you made to each other on your wedding day. Sometime within your life together, and maybe even more often than you think, you will need reminding of the promises you made to each other, to help you through any difficult times you may have to face.

What three things could you do as an individual or a couple to ensure that 'The Big Life' is more successful and longer lasting than 'The Big Day'?

1. ....

2. ....

3. ....

However you choose to plan your day, we suggest you devote more time to 'The Big Life' rather than 'The Big Day'.

Chapter Fourteen

EVERYDAY LIFE

We are going to begin this chapter by asking you a very serious question. What did you, or do you think everyday married life will be like?

When people think about marriage, especially in the fairytale sense of the word, they are generally astonished when they come to realise that ninety-nine percent of marriage is everyday life. The reality of this will set in very quickly after the wedding day or honeymoon if you are fortunate enough to have one. If the reason why you are getting married is to have so called legalised sex, all day, everyday, or to stare lovingly into your spouse's eyes while the bills and washing pile up, you are in for a very rude awakening! Before we discuss the passionate, physical, blood pumping side of relationships within the Green stage, let's take a frank look at the reality of marriage on a day-to-day basis.

When G and I first got married, I took about three weeks off work during the wedding and honeymoon period. At that time I was twenty-three years old and worked in a very target driven and profit crazy organisation. I left work early on the Thursday afternoon and decided to run some last minute errands before the wedding on Monday. As the clock struck 1:30pm I began to feel a sense of freedom and liberation that I was about to begin something totally new and exciting, which would give me a break from the mundane aspects of everyday life for a while. I thought three weeks would feel like a lifetime, but in the end it didn't, it actually felt like a mere three days!

Our wedding day was beautiful, not just in terms of the aesthetics, but rather the fact that he and I promised to be together for life no matter what comes our way, with God as the witness and the anchor. Honestly speaking however, seven years on, it's hard to recall any fine details about it. There were key moments that we will always hold dear but that day in September literally whizzed by and as carefully as we chose, I can guarantee most of the guests don't remember our anniversary because they are living 'everyday life' themselves.

A few days after we got married and before we went on our honeymoon, we went on our first husband and wife date night to Nandos. I went up to order the food while G went to get the cutlery and plates, taking care to wipe everything down one by one with a napkin before the food arrived (my husband seems to have slight OCD). While at the desk, the gentleman asked me "So you've ordered one Lemon and Herb chicken, how spicy would you like the other one?" "Let me just ask my husband" I said, giggling on the inside because it was actually the first time I had referred to him as that, and the notion of that term ever becoming familiar or boring, felt impossible to conceive. So wedded bliss was definitely in the air and we were very much on a major high from the beautiful nuptials we made a few days before. Fast-forward to a few days after we returned from a wonderful stay in the Dominican Republic, and only had a short time to prepare to get back to work. The reality of 'everyday life' became more apparent than it had ever been. We had to make sure our honeymoon clothes were washed, our work clothes were ironed, dinner was cooked, the flat was clean, and we were both attended to. For the first time, I had to do these tasks miles away from where I called home in North West London, at my new home far away from mummy and without her help all the way on the outskirts of London. That day it dawned on me exactly how much my life had actually changed. When I woke up extra early that Monday morning to make a one and a half hour journey on a train, that three weeks ago took seven minutes in a car, it was clear just how different things were, but also just how much had remained the same.

Once you get married, unless you marry a Billionaire, you have the responsibility of going to work and earning a living, just like you did before. However, if you have transitioned from living with mummy, straight into living with your spouse, the type of responsibility placed on you will probably be much higher than previously, as within a relationship both parties need to pull their weight. The things you were able to get away with while living with mummy or daddy will now most probably be a thing of the past. If you lived on your own before getting married, the transition into it may be a little smoother but you will still have to adjust to living with someone else who prefers to wash the dishes just before bedtime rather than straight after each meal. Everyday life as a husband and wife had arrived, and we had no choice but to stand on our own two feet, together.

Because the majority of married life involves things like house work, paying bills, managing finances, going to work, raising children etc, before you get married it is important to define roles, tasks and expectations. For example, knowing that both of us would be working, neither of us thought it would be fair for all the housework to be the responsibility of one person simply because of their gender. Before we were married, G openly admitted he wasn't great with cooking. In order to fix this, and ensure we could have a cooked meal ready when we got home from work in the future, we would play 'Ready, Steady, Cook'. During this time within our Yellow stage, I would practically teach him anything from making cakes all the way to Caribbean cuisine such as Ackee and Salt-fish, even though he is from the deep plains of Africa (well, he actually grew up in South London!). In time his food became on par if not even better than mine. His barbeque chicken is amazing! Defining our roles in the home beforehand, and putting things in place to address any areas, in which either of us lacked a particular skill, meant that the transition into married and everyday life was much smoother.

The following table may be useful to help you define who will generally undertake which tasks. It is also a good idea to mark out the areas in which either of you need further training, so that you will be able and hopefully flexible enough to assume a task at short notice if necessary. You simply need to discuss things with your spouse or future spouse and tick all boxes that apply. If you want your marriage to be as stress free as possible, depending upon your employment circumstances, be careful to ensure that these are divided as equally as possible.

Chore Improvement Table

Chore	Me	Spouse	Me: Further training needed?	Spouse: Further training needed?
Washing up				
Ironing				
Washing clothes				
Cooking				
Vacuuming				
Folding & putting away clothes				

Chores aside, there are more things that come along with everyday life in a marriage. "But he leaves his socks with flakes of dry skin scattered around on the bedroom floor!" Sound familiar? Essentially, if you wait until you are married to move in together, along with becoming husband and wife, you get to experience the running of a home together for the very first time, and experience a feeling of newness and perhaps easily resolved frustration like the scenario above. Dry flakes of skin in dirty socks around the house is simply part of everyday life, you just need to learn two main concepts to making your everyday life a lot easier. These are: the art of compromise, and the ability to pick your battles.

When you say "I do", it is no longer just about you. Whether you realise it or not, by saying those words, you have chosen to consider your spouse in nearly every decision you make. Even small decisions such as whether to buy green grapes this time as opposed to those big juicy plump red grapes you love, or big decisions such as deciding to go back to university for further study, or taking up that speaking engagement in Australia. These all require the thought and consideration of your better half. Decisions that on the surface, seem beneficial for us both financially, like G taking a speaking engagement, may not be such a great idea without considering whether I need a break from the children. Discussing all decisions with your spouse, before taking action, can help your relationship in the short and long term. Buying a mixture of red and green grapes from Waitrose may simply be the perfect solution to your decision-making, where both parties will be happy with their mouthful of grapes, because of the time and effort taken to compromise.

Continuing on with the subject of picking your battles and compromising then, let us introduce 'The Big Brown Tunisian Bag'.

The Big Brown Tunisian Bag

We bought this bag on a trip to Tunisia with my sister and her family and at the time, didn't realise just how valuable it would be in our marriage. It's a big, trendy and real leather bag, the Tunisian gentleman held a lighter to it, in an attempt to prove its authenticity. He told us we were getting it for a good price, but G and my brother-in-law made him give it to them for an even better price.

So what's this bag all about? Well, this is an example of us picking our battles. In our home, I operate a 'clear desk policy' much like one that you would have enforced at your work place, G unfortunately, does not. In the midst of him writing his sermons, life coaching material, and even this manual, the desk tends to get slightly messy, to the point where it is impossible to see what type of wood it is made from. At the end of each day, I say nothing about it, other than to let him know that I am putting all his paper work neatly in 'The Big Brown Tunisian Bag'. Out of sight, out of mind. I get the clear desk, he knows where his work is, and everyone wins! Little things like this, in a lot of relationships, are a major source of contention, where disagreements are blown out of proportion just because of a bit of paper work on a desk. Life is too short to waste energy arguing over silly little things so pick your battles accordingly...

What three issues in my home would be an opportunity for me to demonstrate my ability to compromise, or pick my battles?

1. ....
2. ....
3. ....

"Life is just a journey and I just want to go on that journey with you" This is the journey that I told you G spoke of earlier when he asked me to be his wife. Taking the journey of everyday life with someone you know, love, trust, can compromise with, raise children with, weather storms and have fun with is a beautiful journey indeed. It's a journey that I would not rather be on with anyone else. We pray that you experience something just as great!

Chapter Fifteen

AN EXPRESSION OF LOVE

So now we've talked about 'everyday life', we want to delve a little deeper into the passionate side of a marriage. What are your thoughts surrounding sex and making love? In your mind are they the same thing? Does it depend upon the circumstances in which it takes place? What kind of picture was painted of it when you were young? Was it painted as something dirty and shameful only to be done on a dark night with the lights off in complete secret? Or was it presented as something liberating, allowing you to reach your highest peaks with the blinds ajar without fear of judgement or rejection? Could you talk about it with anyone? What about your mummy and daddy? Were you told to only do it when you're married and then when you got married you didn't have a clue what to do? What if before you entered the Green stage you had multiple partners but your husband has only had one, or even none? What if your views on making love are totally different from your spouse's? What happens when it's taboo to talk about making love with the person you need to make love to? What if you are not quite sure just how and when to use this expression of love or what it was really designed for in the first place? In order for love making to serve its true purpose, both people need to be clear on what that purpose is.

We believe that sex was created by God for the purposes of: procreation and for married couples to feel great and share deep, intimate moments, where two become one. Looking at it holistically, making love is, both parties putting on a performance of what marriage actually is. "A performance?" we hear you question, yes, let us explain this a bit further. Making love to the only person you are deeply in love with and committed to, involves an intense emotional, spiritual and physical connection. It's a place where you should (or in time will) both be comfortable enough to bare all, in terms of your physical nakedness as well your emotional and spiritual attributes. Being vulnerable and completely able to let go is not something that you can do with just anyone. It should be a place where you are both simply 'enough' and feel safe and protected whether you have a body like Halle Berry or a body like Marge Simpson. This performance therefore pertains to the fact that you are acting out the vulnerability that is involved in every day married life, where protection, fun, physical and emotional intimacy, and cherishing your partner, all come into play. The same things we experience in normal, daily, married life finds its way of being acted out in the marital bed or tabletop!

Although making love is not the only expression of love, it is a very good way to keep showing your husband or wife just how you feel about them which we believe needs to come from a place of complete selflessness. In today's society, too much emphasis is placed on 'ensuring that I reach MY climax' and little on the needs and wishes of the other person. Your number one desire should be to make your life partner feel good, fulfilled, special and loved. For that reason, we suggest both parties view love making as a time to serve the needs of their partner. In doing so, you will both always seek to ensure, you are giving the best of yourself, with the ultimate goal being witnessing and contributing all you are to satisfying the person you love.

All of this being said, as individuals of the opposite sex with vastly different life experiences, there can still be complications surrounding your perceptions of love making, which may in turn have an effect on the actual act being successfully initiated or undertaken. If you carry out the following exercises honestly, openly and independently, compare your responses with your spouse if you have one, it may help to open communication channels to improving the sexual dimension of your relationship. If you are single or courting, it may bring about an awareness of your attitude to sex, and the reasons for this, which is knowledge you can apply once you reach the Green stage.

Childhood Thoughts and Feelings About Sex Questionnaire

Finish this statement: My first recollection of talking about sex was when I was ＿＿ years old with ＿＿＿＿＿＿

For each question, please tick either A or B:

1a. Sex was not a taboo subject in my house and I could freely talk about it with my family ☐

1b. I was uncomfortable with discussing sex with my parents and decided to find the information from other sources ☐

2a. Most of my friends were not sexually active before the age of consent ☐

2b. Most of my friends were sexually active before the age of consent ☐

3a. Despite the way sex is portrayed in society, I never felt pressured into having it before I was truly ready ☐

3b. I felt pressured by society into having sex before I was ready and truly understood what it was ☐

4a. I saw the value of waiting to be married to explore sex ☐

4b. I didn't see the point of waiting to be married to explore sex ☐

5a. Based on the experiences of my peers, I viewed sex as sacred ☐

5b. Based on the experiences of my peers I viewed sex as casual ☐

6a. Growing up, teenage pregnancies were seen as a major issue ☐

6b. Growing up teenage pregnancies were not seen as a big deal ☐

7a. As a teenager I was clear on the methods of contraception available ☐

7b. As a teenager I was not clear on all the methods of contraception open to me ☐

8a. Abortion would not have been viewed as a viable option in my circle of friends ☐

8b. Friends of mine viewed abortion as a viable option should they have 'forgotten' to take the appropriate precautions during sexual intercourse or if their contraceptive method failed ☐

9a. I come from a very physically affectionate family ☐

9b. My family seldom express how they feel about me physically or emotionally ☐

10a. I was completely clear on the difference between having sex and making love ☐

10b. I was not clear on the difference between having sex and making love ☐

11a. My self worth has never been tied up in sexual activity ☐

11b. I viewed sex as a way to validate self worth ☐

12a. Whether I did or didn't, I did not find it difficult to wait until I was married to fulfil my sexual desires ☐

12b. Whether I did or didn't, I found it difficult to wait until I was married to fulfil my sexual desires ☐

Once you have completed the test openly and honestly, count up how many A's you have and how many B's you have and write the score in the space below then read the summary pertaining to the score you attained to better understand your childhood sexual thoughts and feelings.

A: ▮▮▮▮ B: ▮▮▮▮

Mostly A's

If you have more A's than you have B's, sex may have been a subject that as a child you were able to talk about freely with your parents. You may not have had a lot of peers that indulged in it before their time and were perhaps not really fazed by the amount of silent pressure that many young people experience to have sex. You may have placed a high value on sex and saw it as revered without being forced by your parents to do so. Teenage pregnancy may have been a major cause for concern and as such you and your core circle of friends may have made sure to be clear on all contraceptive methods ensuring abortion would never have to be an option. Your family may have been adequately affectionate to meet your need to feel loved, so the chances of you mistaking sex for love and searching around for it in other spheres of your life were minimised. Ultimately your self worth appears to come from sources other than those pertaining to sex, and whether or not you waited to have sex, you may not have felt pressured into partaking in the act before you were married.

Mostly B's

If you have more B's than A's, due to sex possibly being a taboo subject within your home, you may have had no choice but to sneakily gather information on sex from other sources. You may have had quite a few friends who were sexually active before the age of consent and felt pressured by society into doing likewise. You may not have seen the point of waiting to be married to engage in sexual activity and subsequently took quite a relaxed approach to the subject. Teenage pregnancies, abortion and lack of contraceptive advice may have all been very common and overlooked in your world. In addition, the physical and emotional family affection that you so desired may not have been available at the time, which could in turn have had an impact on your ability to separate sex and making love. Sex may have been used as a way to validate your self worth and you may have felt pressured into undertaking sexual relations before you were married.

Even Amounts of A's and B's

If you got exactly the same amount of A's and B's it seems that you may have more of a balanced approach to sex. Perhaps you were not too sheltered but at the same time did not over indulge in things of this nature. You may have grown up with an awareness of sex and all that's involved, but didn't always feel the need to partake in it just because your friends did. Sex to you may have been seen as sacred but your rules about having it could have involved simply waiting for that special person rather than having to be married first.

So What Now?

The category you fall into compared to that of your spouse/partner (if you have one) should give you a clearer idea on how similarly or differently you thought about sex growing up. This exercise is not about judgement, but rather about gaining a deeper insight into how our childhood exposure, thoughts and feelings about sex and intimacy may be influencing our attitude to it now. Consider discussing your individual responses with your partner or thinking about it more deeply/discussing things with a friend if you are single. You can even look at these answers as a way to enhance your future or current sexual education and parenting capabilities for your children if you believe that there is a link between sex being a taboo subject in the home and children therefore going to great lengths to find out about it in possibly the wrong way as a result.

So, now that we have looked at childhood influences on our attitude to sex, we will explore our current thoughts/approach to sex within the Green stage.

My Approach to Sex Questionnaire

As mentioned previously, we believe that sex was created by God for procreation and intimacy between married couples only and this questionnaire will be useful for married couples to complete.

All of the statements below are about what you think or what you believe your spouse thinks without asking them first. Tick all that apply then have your spouse repeat this exercise independently and lovingly compare responses.

Bare in mind this is an exercise to identify any areas of improvement, so approach any unexpected responses with this in mind.

For statements 1a-1d, answer in reference to what you believe is the original design for sex.

1a. I understand the reason sex was designed ☐

1b. I do not understand the reason sex was designed ☐

1c. I believe my spouse understands the reason sex was designed ☐

1d. I believe my spouse does not understand the reason sex was designed ☐

2a. I always enjoy sex with my mate ☐

2b. I sometimes enjoy sex with my mate ☐

2c. I seldom enjoy sex with my mate ☐

3a. I think my mate enjoys sex with me ☐

3b. I know my mate enjoys sex with me ☐

3c. I think my mate believes there is room for sexual improvement ☐

4a. My mate seeks to satisfy me above all else ☐

4b. My mate appears to be more interested in satisfying himself or herself ☐

5a. My mate initiates sex more than I do ☐

5b. I initiate sex more than my mate does ☐

5c. We have a balanced approach to initiating sex ☐

6a. Every time we begin to touch each other, it always has to lead to sex ☐

6b. Sometimes we satisfy each other in other ways without the end goal having to be sexual intercourse ☐

7a. My spouse spends enough time on foreplay ☐

7b. My spouse does not spend enough time on foreplay ☐

7c. I spend enough time on foreplay ☐

7d. I do not spend enough time on foreplay ☐

8a. My spouse knows how to read my signals and will respect if I am not in the mood to make love ☐

8b. My spouse goes full steam ahead without checking if I am ready to make love and may be upset if I stop him or her ☐

9a. My spouse hugs and kisses me outside sexual moments ☐

9b. My spouse only hugs and kisses me if he or she wants to have sex ☐

10a. My spouse wants to have sex more than I do ☐

10b. I want to have sex more than my spouse ☐

10c. I believe our sex drives are equal ☐

11a. I am sexually attracted to my spouse ☐

11b. I am not sexually attracted to my spouse ☐

11c. I believe my spouse can make improvements on their physical or emotional attributes so that I can become more attracted to them ☐

12a. I believe my spouse is sexually attracted to me ☐

12b. I believe my spouse is not sexually attracted to me ☐

12c. I believe my spouse thinks I can make improvements on my physical or emotional attributes so that he or she can become more attracted to me ☐

13a. I plan special times to be alone with my spouse ☐

13b. My spouse plans special time to be alone with me ☐

13c. Neither of us plan special alone time ☐

14a. We are both in agreement with the method of contraception we use ☐

14b. We are not in agreement with the method of contraception we use ☐

15a. We are clear on whether we want children, how many we want and the possibility of having to deal with unexpected surprises ☐

15b. We are not clear on whether we want children, how many we want and the possibility of having to deal with unexpected surprises ☐

16a. If we conceived a child at an inconvenient time, abortion would never be an option within our marriage for me ☐

16b. If we conceived a child at an inconvenient time, abortion would be an option within our marriage for me ☐

16c. If we conceived a child at an inconvenient time, I believe abortion would never be an option within our marriage for my spouse ☐

16d. If we conceived a child at an inconvenient time, I believe abortion would be an option within our marriage for my spouse ☐

17a. I am open to trying new things sexually such as sex toys or different positions or locations ☐

17b. I am not open to trying new things sexually such as sex toys or different positions or locations ☐

17c. My spouse is open to trying new things sexually such as sex toys or different positions or locations ☐

17d. My spouse is not open to trying new things sexually such as sex toys or different positions or locations ☐

18a. I can talk freely to my spouse about my sexual likes and dislikes ☐

18b. My spouse will get offended if I tell them I didn't like something they did to me ☐

18c. My spouse can talk freely to me about their sexual likes and dislikes ☐

18d. I tend to get offended if my spouse tells me they didn't like something I did to them ☐

19a. If I don't get to climax, there is no point having sex ☐

19b. If my spouse doesn't get to climax, he or she believes the session was a waste of time ☐

19c. Climaxing is not the most important thing about sex to me ☐

19d. I believe climaxing is not the most important thing about sex to my spouse ☐

20a. I understand that compromise and selflessness needs to be at the forefront of our sexual relationship ☐

20b. I have not fully come to terms with the fact that compromise and selflessness needs to be at the forefront of our sexual relationship ☐

20c. I believe that my spouse understands that compromise and selflessness needs to be at the forefront of our sexual relationship ☐

20d. I do not believe that my spouse understands that compromise and selflessness needs to be at the forefront of our sexual relationship ☐

21. I believe we need to have sex *(Please circle one response)*

More   Less   The Same

22. I believe my spouse thinks we need to have sex *(Please circle one response)*

More   Less   The Same

Answer questions 23 and 24 without speaking to your spouse first and write down your responses. When you have finished ask your spouse questions 25 and 26. Is there a lot of difference between your responses? Talk about this maturely afterwards and give your partner a go at the exercise also!

23. I think the things that tend to put my spouse in a sexual intimate mood are:

a.

b.

c.

24. The things that tend to put me in a sexually intimate mood are:

a.

b.

c.

25. After speaking to them, the things that actually put my spouse in a sexually intimate mood are:

a.

b.

c.

26. After speaking to them, the things my spouse believes tend to put me in a sexually intimate mood are:

a.

b.

c.

Do these questions independently:

27. When rating our current sexual relationship, out of 10 I would give our present stage a

28. If I compare this score to an earlier period in our relationship I believe it has: *(Please circle one response)*

            Declined   Remained the Same   Improved

29. Three things I suggest we do to improve things sexually starting this week are:

a.

b.

c.

30. I understand that sex is just ONE expression of love and other things I could do to show my spouse that I love them are:

a.

b.

c.

Please tick all that apply

31a. I see the value of exploring our individual attitudes to sex and am committed to improving our sexual relationship in anyway possible and will be able and willing to handle an open and loving conversation about this afterwards. ☐

31b. I don't see the value of exploring our individual attitudes to sex and do not wish partake in a discussion about this afterwards. ☐

31c. I believe that my spouse will see the value of exploring our individual attitudes to sex and is committed to improving our sexual relationship in anyway possible and will be able and willing to handle an open and loving conversation about this afterwards. ☐

31d. I don't believe my spouse will see the value of exploring our individual attitudes to sex and may not wish partake in a discussion about this afterwards. ☐

Analysing the Results

Unlike the last exercise on your childhood thoughts and feelings around sex, we believe that the results of this questionnaire should be open to subjective interpretation. We advise that after you have both completed the questionnaire separately, you come together at a relaxed and chilled time, with treats and soothing music in the background to discuss plainly each response, elaborating on reasons for a chosen response where necessary and suggesting ways to improve any concerns that may have arisen. Being aware of the attitude that your spouse has towards your sex lives as well as the attitude they perceive you to have is a very valuable tool that can empower you both, to self reflect and make changes for the better if you wish.

Therefore we have seen throughout the Red, Yellow and Green stages that there are many different ways to express love. Paying special attention to exactly how you do this in the Green stage is a very important factor required for you to attain and maintain the type of relationship you both desire. As discussed, love making between husband and wife should always be enjoyable and the moment it starts to feel like a chore, or is used as a bargaining tool, something is not right. Efforts always need to be made to keep things fresh (especially when children come in the picture) and both parties need to be open and willing to try new things and locations (just don't get arrested!), as you will be making love to each other for the rest of your lives.

"So how should we do it, when should we do it, how often should we do it?" Based on your responses to the previous exercises, you should have a much clearer idea on what the two of you need to do to move forward. Based on the frank nature of some of the questions, careful consideration needs to be taken when discussing the responses, to avoid hurting your partner or causing arguments. Mature relationships however require this type of honesty and the ability to proactively make changes to the areas that need improving in your relationship. The marriage bed should be a place where the world's standards on how and when you should make love has no place, but rather you both decide on a pace and approach that is comfortable within your marriage. Just remember, making love is just one powerful expression of love, freely at your disposal when you are in the Green and most sought after stage. In the safety of a good marriage, continue to express yourselves and to make good love, but also consider other ways you can express love to your spouse. This can include but is not limited to:

- A kiss on the forehead.

- A nature walk.

- Demonstrating patience when dinner isn't ready on time.

- Taking over caring for the screaming baby even though you are shattered yourself.

- Writing a love letter.

- Cooking your spouse's favourite meal.

- Booking them in for a surprise spa treatment.

Other than making love, in what ways does your partner feel loved?

If you don't know, find out practical ways that make your partner feel that you love them and demonstrate it as often as you can! Seek to use an expression of love everyday of your lives together and watch your marriage go from strength to strength.

Chapter Sixteen

THE PITTER PATTER
OF LITTLE FEET

G and I have been blessed with two little boys. We had been together for six years by the time we got married and could have decided to start a family straight away. However we wanted some time to just be a husband and wife before introducing a baby into our world. G and I spoke for a very long time about the life-altering notion of becoming parents. Our talks even before we got married surrounded:

- Whether or not we both wanted children.

- How many children to have.

- When to have them.

- The financial implications of having children.

- The social implications of having children.

- How I would deal with labour.

- Where we would want to raise them.

- How much extended family help would be available.

- The responsibility of growing up a child in a way that would be pleasing to God.

We spoke at length about all aspects of becoming a Mummy and Daddy, even things like childcare arrangements after maternity leave and how we would we be able to survive on one income. When you are fortunate enough to add a child to everyday life, your world will be filled with joy. A great deal of responsibility will also be placed upon your shoulders, as a baby relies on you both to help them navigate every moment of the day, especially in the early years.

Before we were blessed with our children, we baby-sat my niece and nephew who were toddlers at the time, and realised that the time we shared as husband and wife was no longer in the forefront, but seeing to the needs of the children was. Co-parenting involves a lot of sacrifice, so if you are at a place where you are unable to be selfless, perhaps you need to rethink whether parenting at this time is actually a good idea. Some of the sacrifices we have had to make in order for our children to be comfortable are:

- Sleep, sleep and more sleep!!!

- Having one wage in the home so they didn't have to go into mainstream childcare too early.

- Forgoing any luxuries or treats for ourselves so that they could have the basic necessities.

- Not going on holidays or dates as often as before.

- Participating in activities that you are not necessarily comfortable doing, like daddy taking them every week to a baby club that is full of breastfeeding mums. (Where does one look?!)

- Having someone else to consider in every single decision we made.

One thing we refuse to sacrifice as parents though, is our dreams. In order to pursue them with children on board, you need to be very disciplined, this is why I am up at 5am writing this chapter before I hear "Mummy, Mummy, Mummy, brekkie please!" coming from their room as they jump on the bed with terrible morning breath. We are mindful that we are their first educators and the people they look up to, for an example to follow. Showing children that with: strength, skill, prayer and discipline, it is possible to achieve your dreams, is a very important aspect of being an example. Having children and managing all the different stages from here to adulthood will continue to add a new, exciting and probably sometimes challenging and frustrating dimension to our lives.

THE COLOURS OF LOVE

Three things we need to consider before having children are:

1. ....

2. ....

3. ....

Three changes that may occur once we have children are:

1. ....

2. ....

3. ....

Three things we can do to not loose sight of us as individuals and as a couple are:

1. ....

2. ....

3. ....

So as you can see, we considered almost every eventuality pertaining to birthing and raising children, however, one thing we never envisioned experiencing was knowing first hand what it would feel like to loose a child.

It was an evening in May 2009 and we had been trying for a baby for a very short time. I sneaked in the home bathroom after work to take a pregnancy test and was shocked to see that on the little white stick, there was a positive red line. I called G to the kitchen and nonchalantly left it on the brown wooden worktop in an attempt for him to unexpectedly find out the good news. He was peacefully happy but looking back I remember feeling unsure, as although there was a positive red line starring back at us from the kitchen counter, it was extremely faint. Faint or not, it was still a positive line as assured by the nurse after I went to Accident and Emergency with mild abdominal pain. As time progressed we were excited but also a little scared, as this was something we had never experienced before and we wondered if we had the tools necessary to raise a child as our own. Fast forward a few weeks, we kept the news to ourselves and nursed each other emotionally as the pains got worse and the hospital visits got more frequent. With all the negative reports from the doctors, and having to smile to mask my pain at work, we knew what was coming; we were just not ready nor willing to face it. We hoped and prayed that the blood tests were wrong, that the nurses were wrong and that we were not about to loose our baby. *Cupcake* was slipping away right before our eyes, and we were powerless to stop it, and it seemed for a moment that the God who was in control of it all, would. After cleaving together and randomly tearfully opening bible passages such as Isaiah 43:19 (NLT) which says '*For I am about to do something new. See, I have already begun! Do you not see it? I will make a pathway through the wilderness. I will create rivers in the dry wasteland.*' We had our hopes dashed as we felt that God should and would fix *this* situation, but **fortunately** He didn't, at least He didn't do so in the way we thought He should. Humanly speaking, we were in pieces and wanted *Cupcake* to survive, not to be given another baby, we wanted *this* baby! But what if *this* baby wasn't well? What if God allowing us to give birth to this baby would mean a life of turmoil? What if He allowed me to progress further through the pregnancy and my life was now at risk? Romans 8:28 (NLT) was all we had to hold onto: '*And we know that God causes everything to work together for the good of those who love God and are called according to His purpose for them.*' We were steadfast in this belief: somehow, God would make this work out for our good.

After many tears, a holiday abroad, soaking ourselves in each other and the promises littered throughout God's word, we were stronger than ever and ready to allow new hope, fresh perspective and possibly a new baby into our lives. We treasured each other now more than ever before and understood that the ability to partake in the giving of life was one that was a privilege not to be taken lightly. I did everything in my power health wise to make my body a nice place for a baby to live and left the rest to God. After choosing not to transfer any negative thoughts about the loss of *Cupcake* onto this new journey with *Little Bear*, His peace carried us through ten months of pregnancy, an emergency C-section and beyond! Even better, just over two years later, totally unexpectedly and in a time where we were not considering adding any more children to our family just yet, God surprised us with another little bun in the oven! We believe that this was God's way of replenishing a hundred fold what was taken away. Having our second son totally changed our quality of life in unimaginable ways and has afforded us luxuries that could only be possible by a move of God.

With the pitter patter of little feet, see them as a blessing and trust God to help you look after them, after all, He is the Life Giver and knows what He is doing and He stays awake watching them whilst you are fast asleep! As a fulfilled Homemaker, Masters Student, Executive Pastor, Songwriter and Super Happy Wife, financially it doesn't need to make sense on paper, for it to make sense with God!

Children are a blessing from God, if you do choose to have them; they have the ability to make everyday life with your spouse a little less mundane. The tricky part is ensuring you still make enough time for your spouse, so you remain life partners that are very much in love, and in tune with each other, as opposed to parents that simply pass each other in the hallway. It is possible to maintain an extremely happy Green stage with children, do it properly and you'll have a heavenly marriage and someone to look after you both in your old age!

Chapter Seventeen

ZONE ONE

Picture this, it's a hot summer's evening, the kind of evening that have people all across the city in shorts and t-shirts having a cold drink after work, those evenings when children are outside chasing ice cream vans down their streets. This was a picture perfect English summer evening, when everyone seemed at peace with themselves and with each other. In the offices of a local Church Pastor, the mood was very different. A married couple of four years had come in to talk to their Pastor.

"Why are you considering the option of going your separate ways?" the Pastor enquired.

"Because all my husband wants is to have sex," the wife replied.

"Most women would be pleased!" said the Pastor.

"They are!" the wife fired back. **"That's why I want a divorce."**

Throughout this manual, we have been exploring and will continue to explore various ways to enjoy healthy romantic relationships, enhance and build good foundations for a great married life. However the unfortunate reality for many, is that their marriage is left exposed to various external factors, influences and opportunities to destroy in the blink of an eye, what has taken years to build up.

Many marriages become unhealthy, cold, stagnant, and end in divorce, because there hasn't been an intentional agreement to do everything necessary to protect the marriage. Infidelity is one of the greatest stressors to any marriage, as it breaks the bond of trust, commitment and faithfulness to your spouse. However, other stressors also include extended family interference in your marriage, pornography, and friends, just to name a few.

According to statistics, over forty-five percent of marriages in the UK end in divorce, with well over half of those occurring within the first decade of marriage. Most of us don't have to think twice about taking out insurance for our cars, homes, dogs and iPads, yet we fail to take the necessary precautions when it comes to fail-proofing our marriages.

In a marriage, both the husband and wife must be intentional about protecting their relationship, by controlling what they permit to enter their 'circle of love'. Selone and I refer to this as 'Zone One'. The Zone One concept is a concept that takes its lead from the London Underground system, which is divided into travel zones. Zone One represents the central London area. This area includes some of the most iconic, tourist, business, and government districts of our great city, and in respect to potential threats, is probably the most protected. If you are travelling in from other parts of the city, you will be required to purchase an extension on your travel card or Oyster in order to travel within the zone.

Properties in Zone One are far more expensive than any other areas of London. It is a Zone of value, of great worth, and therefore receives great protection. If we constantly view our marriages as 'Zone One', we would take greater care and place more emphasis on protecting it from 'outsiders' and 'outside stressors' that can have a negative impact on our marriages.

Zone One must consist of three people alone, you, your spouse and God. Remember, God should be the centrepiece of your marriage union. Marriage is and will always be God's great idea! Zone One must be a place where secrets are kept, where trust resides, and where a husband and wife feel safe and secure.

We all have friends and family members who we tell everything to, however in marriage, you have to be cautious of who you talk to about what happens in your marriage. If a small disagreement between you and your spouse, which can often be resolved in a short time, gets in the ear of someone external to your marriage, it can be misconstrued as a major flair up, this can cause gossip to spread like wild fire, and for your spouse to be looked upon with great suspicion and rejection by others. This also makes the process of mending things a lot harder, especially since it should have been none of the external person's business in the first place. If every single day of your life, your husband bought you flowers and one day he stupidly decided to tell you to

"Shut up!", people will always remember and hold onto the one negative thing he has done. Decide carefully whether it is wise to involve other people in a union that was created only for the two of you.

The Zone One notion is very powerful indeed. We've witnessed couples that have had an episode of infidelity and were on the verge of divorce, rebuilding the walls of their marriage and starting over again. By using the Zone One strategy, intentionally analysing the threats and weaknesses of their marriage and also making a conscious effort to re-commit to building up their trust and love again, miracles have happened.

Zone One; protect your marriage with everything you are.

Chapter Eighteen

PRESERVING THE FRESHNESS

In order for any relationship to work, grow and thrive, it requires constant effort from both people involved. Of all the stages previously explored in this manual, marriage needs even more effort for a state of happiness to be maintained.

In a marriage, it is easier to get caught up in routines, neglect each other, and allow the cares of everyday living to take control. This can result in a cold, predictable and sluggish union. Marriage at its core should be the most amazing and thrilling adventure any two individuals can experience. Whether you've been married for three months, two years, or sixty years, the married couple must be intentional about constantly working on their marriage, and exploring new ways to 'spice things up'. This helps to avoid things becoming dim, and falling into a state of mediocrity, or worse, both or one of the partners looking to external sources to fulfil their needs. When you're familiar with your spouse, you see them at their best, and, at their worst. This may include but is not limited to: spot cream, house clothes, missing weave tracks, black roots and peroxide blond hair, headscarfs on twenty-four seven, an unshaven face, shaving bumps on the back of the neck and a three week old hair cut. When a Beyonce or Justin Timberlake look alike comes around your way, you need to think twice about how much you stand to loose. Whenever there are issues within a marriage, individuals must think carefully about the consequences of confiding in someone else of the opposite sex, as at that moment they may seem a far better option than their spouse. Never mistake fantasy for reality; oftentimes affairs of this kind are exactly that, a fantasy that can leave you with nothing. A stale marriage is never an excuse to cheat on your partner. However, being mindful of these facts and making a conscious effort to keep things fresh is important, as infidelity is a very hard wound to heal. This is because it has the potential to destroy trust and bring about insecurity. Trust and security form part of the basis for any good relationship, if we have no trust, we really have nothing else.

In trying to preserve the freshness in a marriage, another point to consider is the experience of love. Love by itself is never enough to make a relationship work. The divorce courts are full of people who love each other. The key to having a healthy, happy, great relationship is to intentionally cultivate & maintain The Experience of Love. Couples need to ensure that their spouse feels loved, accepted and appreciated. When you take your spouse for granted, and are overly critical of them, walls of protection tend to go up which creates a cycle of conflict, and a cold and distant atmosphere. It's easier said than done, but if you value what you have, making the effort to stay on top of this, would be a top priority. You don't want to let your well run dry before you realise you miss your water.

One thing that both husbands and wives whine about when their marriage hits the rocks or they feel a sense of detachment, is they feel they are either being taken for granted, or there is no longer that sense of freshness, excitement or adventure. The key to keeping a marriage fresh and exciting, is for both hubby and wifey to add as many fresh and exciting dimensions, and doing so as often as possible. This is not rocket science, nor is it quantum physics, but sometimes couples can seem at a loss as to what they need to do to change things. Here are a few suggestions:

Date Nights

One of the simplest things you can do both for yourself and for the life of your marriage is to plan a date night at least once a week, ensuring that you both have it in your diaries. You might be wondering, how can I date the person I'm married to? Well, you better! Otherwise you run the risk of co-existing in a dry and lethargic marriage, that has lost it's will to live.

Date nights are a great opportunity for you both just to be together, alone, remembering why you first fell in love, sending the signal out to your spouse that they do still matter! Therefore it is strongly recommended, that despite all the pressures, bills, children, commitments, work and all other important everyday things a couple must juggle in their married life, that the couple must make time to date each other!

Remember those things you did together before the wedding? Before the kids came along? Before that new job? Before the mortgage? Well, you need to keep doing them in your marriage. Catch a new film at the cinema, get out to

China Town and watch the world go by, take a walk by The Embankment, book a table at your favourite restaurant, play on your Nintendo Wii together, take silly pictures at a phone booth, look through your wedding pictures, play knock down ginger or simply walk hand in hand around your neighbourhood, reminiscing about your first kiss. You'll be surprised how great simple things such as date nights are to adding life and freshness to a marriage.

The value of getting all dressed up to go out on a date with your spouse is often underestimated. When my baby and I go out on our date nights, it is exciting watching her put on a classy dress and heels, and just being able to sit across a candle-lit table in a restaurant with the most beautiful woman on God's earth! After seeing her in house clothes most of the time, it's a nice reminder of just how beautiful and awesomely hot she really is. Thank you Jesus!

Apart from the scheduled dates already in your diaries, it would be great to also surprise your spouse by calling them out of the blue at work or at home and telling them to cancel all their plans for the evening or weekend, and surprise them with a candle lit dinner, lunch on a boat, a spa break or something even simple as a walk in the park. As human beings, we all love surprises every once in a while, it makes our hearts skip a beat; it makes us feel alive and excited. Every marriage must have these elements in order to grow stronger and stay fresh.

If, like us, you have children you may be thinking 'How can we have date nights with our kids to take care of?' There are ways to manage this, you can arrange for a baby sitter, family members, neighbours, or close friends to look after the children. Also to ensure you have the finances to go on those all important date nights, it would be great to incorporate costs of date nights in your monthly budget planning, so you can ensure it is a priority for you both, as opposed to an afterthought.

Joint Projects

Another thing to explore when looking for ideas to add freshness to your marriage is to do projects together. Both of you have qualities and gifts that can be utilised in putting together anything from a simple project to a business venture. One project could be redecorating your home, where each of you has allocated tasks. Recently, we undertook a home renovation project on our property where my wife took charge of the interior decorating, colour schemes, furniture purchases, and I took charge of getting in the builders, painting, and buying all the tiling and floorings. It was an entire month of excitement, mainly because it was something we were doing together. When expecting a new baby, this can also be a project that you both can be part of, in terms of buying beddings, clothing or even putting together the birthing plan.

Joint projects have the ability to show you how well you work together as a team. You may have some improvements to make, or you may sail through it without any glitches, either way, it would have been something you decided to do together. It will also allow you both to take time away from the everyday routine of marriage, work and family. This can ignite the spark that your marriage needs, or ensure your marriage doesn't fall into a state of stagnation. Other ideas for joint projects could be planning your next holiday, starting a new business (which could also provide you with another income stream, that might just help alleviate some of those financial strains), choosing schools for the kids, going to the gym together, or as simple as planning the weekly food shopping together. You'll be surprised how much these small changes can inject life into your marriage.

Compliments

We all like to be complimented on our new haircuts, our new shoes, and our culinary skills in the kitchen. It does the world of good for our self-esteem to know that someone else acknowledges that we have done something well. Therefore, on a daily basis, find one thing to compliment your spouse about.

In a marriage, another way of complimenting our spouse is by continuing to 'woo' each other by giving presents that are not associated with birthdays or anniversaries. Surprise gifts on the way home from work have a way of reminding your spouse that he or she really matters to you. It can be as simple as buying their favourite brand of chocolate malted milk biscuits or as expensive as a five star all-inclusive trip to Paris. Don't wait for your spouse to prompt you for a compliment before you give it. Make it your daily mission to say something complimentary to your partner and best friend, even if it's a simple "You look nice." The thing to be mindful of, is that none of us know when we will breathe our last breath, and doing things like this regularly, will minimise the chance of having regrets about not appreciating your spouse as much as possible while they are still here.

Be Silly!

Life, especially marriage can be so serious at times. It is good to find something silly to do together. It could be something you both enjoyed from your childhood, such as playing WWF wrestling on the sofa or walking in on your spouse while in the shower and writing 'I love you' on the steamy shower glass, mirrors or window. Be creative and find something silly to do together that will make you both laugh, and most importantly make you laugh together.

It is vital that in order to keep your marriage fresh and exciting, that you remember why you fell in love in the first place. Keep those butterfly feelings close at all times. If you ever find yourself or both of you slipping into a rut, simply be creative and mix things up a little. You are life partners; you're in this marriage 'until death do us part.' Therefore enjoy each other every day, and you will be so much happier together with each day that passes.

If you are married or planning to get married, what kind of dates could you schedule just for you and your spouse?

1. ....

2. ....

3. ....

What joint projects could you see yourself doing with your spouse?

1. ....

2. ....

3. ....

Make a list of other ideas that you could utilise to ensure your marriage stays fresh. Even if you're not yet married, this will be a good list to take into your future marriage and share with your wife/husband when setting marriage expectations during courtship.

1. ....

2. ....

3. ....

4. ....

5. ....

Like a piece of tin foil wrapped over a nicely home baked meal, do everything in your power to make the Green stage a happy place, preserve the freshness with everything you have.

Chapter Nineteen

MONEY MATTERS

We hear it all the time, million dollar athletes or musicians declared bankrupt, or working class families struggling to feed the children each week. Sometimes the working class families actually end up with more money at the end of the day than those who have millions at their disposal. So what's the issue here? Level of income? Not necessarily. In actual fact, it's to do with expenditure and how people in these two types of scenarios choose to manage their money. It's not necessarily how much you have, it's what you do with what you have! Money is a gravely important issue that can make for a very happy or very sad relationship.

Just the other day, G and I were driving through the area we lived in when we first got married. We happened to go past a specific open plain with a very large hill and a serene view of the surroundings. As we continued to drive past, I quickly glanced up the hill, to the left, and near the Oak tree, seeking out a particular bench we used to frequent. This wasn't just any bench, it was the bench that was used to hash out all the unsaid words and the difficulties we had communicating in the house in the very early stage of our marriage. G reminded me that this was the bench we would sit on when I was 'getting on at him' about how he managed his finances. Where he would behave like an ostrich, preferring to bury his head in the sand rather than face the potential reality of money mismanagement. Money matters are serious enough to make or break a marriage. This is why we believe we need to address the problems we encountered relating to money, and the solutions we developed together to fix them.

During my childhood, I had been taught very good money management skills from my Mum, about not living beyond my means, working hard to purchase 'needs' rather than 'wants' and saving for my future. Throughout my late teens and early twenties, I always had a steady job while completing my education, but unfortunately I neglected to apply these pearls of wisdom. I was used to making and spending my money as I pleased. After realising, however, that at the end of every month, I actually had less in my account than I thought I should, and was unable to account for where this hard earned cash had actually disappeared, I decided to make some changes. I backtracked and adopted all the pearls of wisdom my mother taught me, and incorporated a practical method of using an excel spreadsheet to account for the following on a monthly basis:

- Income

- Expenditure

- Exact details of monthly bills and the amounts required

- Savings

- Disposable income

For this sheet to remain accurate, I had to be disciplined enough to update it every single time I spent money from my account. This included everything from the purchase of a winter coat from H&M for £39.99, to a Happy Meal of £1.99 from McDonalds. That way, by adding in specific formulas in advance, the excel sheet would automatically calculate exactly how much disposable income I had left, after all bills were paid and each spend was accounted for. At any given moment, I knew what was in my account to the penny and never had to deal with the embarrassment of having my card declined at the Topshop till, or was never ever hit with fees for being overdrawn. Sounds great right? Well, I thought so too, however, trying to get G to adopt the same way of thinking and selling him all the benefits of my so called 'finance sheet', was much much harder than I anticipated. Thankfully, I adopted these practices before we got married which is why as I mentioned earlier, saving for the wedding was extremely easy. However, although G was half on board, the other half of him wanted to remain a big fat bird that couldn't fly with his head under the earth for as long as possible. For him, the Finance Sheet just forced him to face the uncomfortable, harsh reality of exactly how much we 'didn't' have after all the bills were paid. At this point, we felt it necessary to revisit some questions to evaluate our attitudes to money, that we had asked each other in the past. Maybe you can try it, by yourself, and then with your spouse:

Financial Check:

Rate your thoughts about money from 1 (Strongly Disagree) to 5 (Strongly Agree)

1. Money is for spending ☐

2. Money is for saving ☐

3. Our financial priorities are being cared for ☐

4. It is important to live on a budget ☐

5. I think it is acceptable to borrow money (Credit) to have the finer things in life ☐

6. Sorting out our finances is/would be my spouses job ☐

7. I would be happy to ask for financial support from my in-laws ☐

8. My money is my money to use as I see fit ☐

9. Financial plans have been made for the future ☐

10. If we got into financial difficulties we would both cut down on expenditure ☐

11. I don't want my spouse to know the true state of my finances ☐

12. I would like to manage the family finances ☐

13. I would prefer my spouse to handle the family finances ☐

14. The scale of our wedding day is likely to mean/meant that we start/started married life in debt ☐

Expectations about how money is handled may differ widely from your spouse/partner and the possibility for disagreement is high. That was definitely the case for us, but eventually, we were able to reach a common ground. Therefore, following many sunsets after work on that particular park bench, G was able to see that being responsible, and on the same page about how we managed our finances, was imperative to achieving certain things in the future. For example, purchasing a bigger family home when we have children, or being able to go on holiday as and when we pleased or simply being able to buy fresh fruit at the market without our card being declined at the ATM machine. He began to understand that it was not about me trying to control his money, but rather me trying to put things in place for us both to have a comfortable and steady future.

The agreement then became that I would manage the family finances and he would simply tell me how much he spent, and on what, and I would create and maintain a finance sheet for him, always giving him an accurate picture of his disposable income. G understood that this was never about me telling him what he could or couldn't buy, but rather advising him on how to keep more of all he earned. Now, this method still works extremely well for us, and G, the convert, will happily tell you all the benefits of being committed to the finance sheet system. Whether or not it works for you, will depend upon both parties understanding the importance of not keeping financial secrets, having a desire to maximise the finances you do have, and being disciplined to update the sheet on a regular basis. This system may also be useful for a single person who wants to get their finances in order before they encounter that special moment with their future mate.

Here is an example of our Finance Sheet adjusted to 'Rachel and Ryan's' budget:

Rachel's Finance Sheet Example

Date	Wages	Bill/ Expense	Amount	Total Expenditure	Disposable Income
31.02.2012	£1654.23	Mortgage	£687.21	£1509.71	£144.52
		Food shopping	£150.00		
		Tithe	£166.00		
		Insurance	£42.70		
		Travel	£153.60		
		Council tax	£148.00		
		Sky	£52.20		
		O2	£30.00		
		Date night	£30.00		
		Holiday savings	£50.00		

As mentioned earlier, this finance sheet has worked very well for our family in terms of being on top of our family finances. You can create one of your own that works well for you and your family. Debt, financial secrets, financial arguments and frivolous spending are all now a thing of the past within our home. In today's society, it's probable that you will never ever feel as though you have enough. If you can manage properly what you do have, it will save you a lot of issues in your marriage, and has the ability to make your family feel like you are all billionaires.

Here are a few biblical principles that have helped us manage our money better, you may find them useful also:

You shall remember the Lord your God, for it is He who gives you power to get wealth, that He may confirm His covenant that He swore to your fathers, as it is this day. (Deuteronomy 8:18 ESV)

Keep your life free from love of money, and be content with what you have, for He has said, "I will never leave you nor forsake you." (Hebrews 13:5 ESV)

Bring the full tithe into the storehouse, that there may be food in My house. And thereby put Me to the test, says the Lord of hosts, if I will not open the windows of heaven for you and pour down for you a blessing until there is no more need. (Malachi 3:10 ESV)

"Do not lay up for yourselves treasures on earth, where moth and rust destroy and where thieves break in and steal, but lay up for yourselves treasures in heaven, where neither moth nor rust destroys and where thieves do not break in and steal. For where your treasure is, there your heart will be also. (Matthew 6:19-21 ESV)

And this same God Who takes care of me will supply all your needs from His glorious riches, which have been given to us in Christ Jesus. (Philippians 4:19 NLT)

Money matters sorted in our household? CHECK! What about yours?

Chapter Twenty

LIFE'S CURVEBALLS

With all the planning, preparation and crossed fingers in the world, oftentimes, life can, and will throw curveballs. Curveballs within the context of a marriage or relationship, can either strengthen or break the couple involved. Curveballs are those situations and scenarios that arise unexpectedly, and are often things we never imagined could happen to us! Situations can arise ranging from work related stress, long term illness, infidelity, miscarriage, bereavement, financial constraints, job loss, and so much more. Some people dismiss the possibility of anything negative ever happening to them in their relationship. Their idea of married life is one filled with nothing but rose petals, walking by the river hand in hand, two kids by each side, well paying jobs, and a 'happily ever after' ending. Indeed, this is the ideal, and it is good to approach marriage with optimism, but we must also be aware that 'life' can happen, it can blind-side us and throw us curveballs that we just were not ready to catch.

Not many things in life are certain, but unless you are a fictional character in a romance novel, it is likely that there will be a time when a couple will face unanticipated scenarios in their relationship, that places a huge strain on their way of being. Not every curveball that life throws has to end negatively or be allowed to destroy a relationship. One key to managing these situations is to expect the unexpected, fuelling each day with love and laughter. This will enable you to generate enough 'love fuel' in the good times that will sustain you through the tough times.

At times, curveballs test the authenticity of a partnership. A relationship, and in some instances a marriage, is proven to possess no authenticity if it has no staying power to overcome a curveball, or a negative situation. Simply because a relationship looks 'all together' on the surface, does not mean it has a strong core. This is why it is extremely vital for couples to ensure they are committed to building a strong foundation, and constantly investing in strengthening the core of their relationship as expressed in the Red and Yellow stages. Celebrities often inspire people to want the type of relationship they display on screen, or on the pages of glossy magazines. Unfortunately, a great deal of celebrities' relationships end in breakups or scandal. This is something that frequently fills the gossip pages of newspapers, and is written about by online bloggers. Having a relationship that looks good on the outside does not necessarily mean it has the core strength on the inside to withstand the storms of life and the adverse situations that marriages are not immune from.

One of the amazing things about being in a loving marriage is to have a partner to weather the storms of life with, and be a combined force field to hit back at the testing curveballs. Marriages are supposed to provide an impenetrable shelter and refuge, a safe place, a refreshing place, a place of peace. Marriage should be a place where you experience guaranteed safety and renewed strength, even while everything else is falling apart around you. It's also important both persons ask themselves, "Can we handle the uncertainties of life together?" "Are we built on something authentic enough to outlast the storms that life could potentially throw at us?"

It has often been said and proven that whatever the foundation a house is built upon, will determine how it fairs in the event of turbulent weather, or adverse environmental conditions. The same is true of a marriage that wants to last forever.

So how should you handle curveballs? One of the key ingredients to handling curveballs is making up your minds, and coming to an agreement before a crisis, that even if you are pitched a curveball, you'll both still choose to hit a 'home run' together! It's similar to the old, cliché-like, but yet so powerful rhetoric, 'If life throws you eggs, make omelettes'. You need to try your utmost to make the best of a bad situation. If one partner is feeling weak, the other one will need to assume the position of Coach who is able to remind you both of the pact you made, and their belief that, after you have been pressed by the fire, you will come out on the other side as pure, shiny and powerful gold. Being able to defeat difficult situations as they arise, will seldom materialise however, if one partner assumes a 'retreat and surrender' attitude, and doesn't tap into their inner strength and faith, to answer the door when fear comes knocking. Curveballs have the ability to drive a couple apart, make them act like they are on opposing teams, or even worse, encourage them to perceive each other as the greatest terrorists in their lives. During these tough times, a united front is extremely important.

Amos 3:3 (NLT) says, *"Can two people walk together without agreeing on the direction?"*

Division within a marriage, in good times or bad will ensure that nothing good is ever accomplished. Even if, in the end, the worst does happen, at least you can both hold your heads up high, knowing that you didn't go down without a fight, and that you fought, together. When you have committed to ensuring that your marriage is for life, and that you are both responsible for ensuring the security and longevity of it, a greater sense of stability will arise. This allows for a lesser propensity to be 'shaken and stirred' by the situations of life.

As a couple, my wife and I hold firmly to a scripture in our favourite book, which states: *"Though one may be overpowered, two can defend themselves. A cord of three strands is not quickly broken"* (Ecclesiastes 4:12 NLT). Building a forever-lasting marriage has a pre-requisite of ensuring it is built on strong, solid foundations. Therefore, not only is coming together important in hard times but having a strong source to anchor your faith is an absolute necessity. We believe that when a man and woman come together, they are stronger when God is invited to be the centrepiece of their marriage, and the 'third strand' of the cord. This understanding allows couples to have a greater strength and sense of security necessary to overcome potholes, roadblocks, and stormy weathers in their marriage. Especially in times when they are feeling weak, they are able to rely on a God who is always strong who beckons us to give him the burdens we carry so that He can fix them for us.

Communication is also a great tool that enables couples to 'keep on ticking, even while their marriage is taking a licking'. Curveballs often cause couples to go into solitary isolation from each other, and you're left with a house where neither person is talking to each other, the bedroom is cold, and the atmosphere grows ever more toxic. Make it a duty for both of you to engage in conversation, communicate with your bodies, communicate with a smile and spend time together. The last thing you want is for your relationship to be torn apart because of something you both went through. Open and honest yet optimistic communication is vital for any relationship facing upheaval in their home.

Another way of handling the curveballs is to simply take a break, and get away from it all, together, and give yourselves an opportunity to be refreshed and reinvigorated. Any activity that allows you to disengage from the curveball experience for a while, such as: a short stay at a spa, a weekend away, an exotic long haul holiday, a visit to the cinema, or just walking the dogs together, can help you cope with the current situation. Try to step into an environment that is tranquil. The break may allow a fresh perspective and encourage the flow of new strategies, placing you closer to overcoming your seemly unmoveable mountain.

In addition to this, constantly reaffirm each other with positive words, positive language and reassurance of your commitment. Curveballs can leave a couple feeling deflated, under-valued, guilty, lonely, and troubled with a sense of low self esteem, therefore it is important to elevate your spouse's self perception and mood, by affirming and reaffirming them. For example, showering them with compliments, serving them through every day chores, cooking dinner, constantly talking to them about how much you appreciate them, writing a positive post about your spouse on social media that celebrates them, and not playing the blame game or seeking to tear them down.

Life is full of uncertainties and situations that can throw a marriage off course if care is not taken. On this journey, things can and will often go wrong, but you can choose not to allow these situations to have a negative impact on your relationship. Marriage is a great investment; therefore ensure that you are investing greatly into it, even in lean times. You'll both reap the rewards of a Green stage that lasts, and stands the test of time and adversities.

When curveballs are shooting through the air at high speed, aiming at your marriage, get your Green bat out and keep on hitting!

Chapter Twenty-one

ANALYSE THIS

Many of us have rightly subscribed to the great benefits associated with getting regular health check ups. Many of us even ensure that at least once a year, or before the winter months creep in, we get our cars checked, to ensure they have the right oil levels, the wheels are aligned, and the brakes are working. Just like a healthy body, and a well-oiled car, our marriages can do with regular health checks. The reality is that most married folks take their marriages and their partners for granted. After saying "I do", and returning from honeymoon, you'll be surprised how many couples fall back into the crazy pace of life, the rat race, kids, families, friends, church, Sunday morning football and spending hours on the Xbox, only with a new partner by their side. Tragically, the freshness of their marriage wears off, and the couple start to slip into familiarity. They stop noticing each other, and feelings of resentment, questions about desirability and irritation about the small things, start to set in.

As everyday life takes hold, some couples, intentionally or not, begin to put other things before their spouse, such as, work, children or personal hobbies and don't actually realise that their marriage is in trouble. Believe it or not, sometimes people only arrive at the realisation that they need to start making changes that breathe new life into their 'dying' or 'struggling' marriage, when their spouse has sought the advice of a divorce lawyer. No one signs up for a mediocre marriage, or a married life that's just 'doing OK!' This type of mindset leads to the slippery road of boredom, and opens up the marriage to an overflow of marital threats. Every married couple should have a desire and intentionality about them, to make their marriage a life-long experience of what happens when heaven kisses earth! Failure to regularly perform a health check on a marriage, will mean a couple could be sinking like the Titanic, without realising it until they are fully submerged under water, in a shark infested ocean, without any rafts or life boats in sight. It is critical for real honesty and transparency between couples, to ensure that they are able to identify any threats to their marriage, and quickly identify solutions, or put up necessary barriers to ensure longevity and happiness in their union.

In the world of business, it is critical, whether a new start up, an established company stepping into a new market, or any business organisation with a desire to survive and thrive in their market, to conduct an initial or regular structured planning process known as SWOT Analysis. The SWOT analysis, credited to Albert Humphrey of the Stanford Research Institute (1960), evaluates the degree to which both the internal and external environment of an organisation affects the current or projected future of a product or organisation. It identifies and evaluates the Strengths, Weaknesses, Threats and Opportunities involved in the project, product or business venture.

Over the years, we have been able to adapt this process to helping couples, including ourselves, identify our own strengths and weaknesses, which are internal to us, making strategic observations of potential threats and opportunities, ensuring we adjust accordingly. When a couple is able to invest the time necessary to take an objective and collaborative approach to utilising the SWOT analysis in their marriage, it has the capacity to enhance their life experience. There are so many benefits associated with performing a regular health check on your marriage, which will enable you to enjoy rather than endure your marriage. At the epicentre of these benefits is the fact that it enables and empowers couples to make corrections and realign their marriage before love leaves the building, and ends up at the front door of a family solicitor about to read through the signed pre-nuptial agreement.

So how do you implement the basic theory of a SWOT analysis into the life of your forever after?

It is encouraged that a SWOT analysis is carried out once every quarter by both the husband and wife. This has to be at a time set aside with no other distractions or external stresses, straining on your reflection time together.

Strengths:

Both of you should take some time to step back, recall and write down the things you have achieved together as couple such as the wins you've encountered together, and because of each other. This helps emphasise the great advantages of your married life together. Talk through the things you've weathered as a team. You might even give each other a kiss at this moment, to celebrate the fact that you have good points and great wins in your relationships (cheesy we know!). A great philosopher once said that 'What you never celebrate will never grow'. Therefore it is vital that you celebrate the wins in your marriage, regularly! Then identify the positives in terms of how you make each other feel.

All the above will help draw up a snapshot of what makes up the strengths of your marriage. The key is, to work together to come up with ways and intentional decisions you'll make individually and together to capitalise on those wins. You need to also discuss how to keep improving on them to enhance the experience you both enjoy within your marriage.

Weaknesses:

Weaknesses are those areas that you as individuals, and together as a couple struggle with, which have or have the potential to hinder your marriage. These struggles could include: poor communication, lack of respect and time spent together, poor management of finances, conflicting parenting styles, different expectations about sex or not having adequate boundaries in place which leaves your marriage penetrable by external parties. As difficult as it is to sometimes talk about weaknesses, it is vital that every couple identifies, and comes to terms with their weaknesses in order to find fruitful ways of tackling them together. You might find that some weaknesses such as handling finances might take a longer period of time to come to grips with, but it is essential for the survival of the marriage, to minimise the impact it has on your lives together, and the family.

Opportunities:

Every married couple should be able to identify details about the uniqueness of their spouse, and their relationship together. Identify dispositions, gifts and even quirkiness that make you both tick. In these, might lay opportunities to build something great together or embark on a trip or business venture together. Opportunities can also take the form of things happening in the wider world around you, that as a couple, you can take advantage of in order to grow your marriage. For instance, holiday seasons are great opportunities to arrange a quick couple's or family getaway, to help refresh your marriage, while getting away from the everyday mundane activities of life! One partner may be gifted in writing and may need some encouragement to turn a hobby into a book writing venture. Always be on the look out for opportunities that will enhance you as a couple, opportunities that will help you both express and refresh your love for each other, and safeguard your marriage.

Threats:

Watch out for small foxes! The wisest man to have ever lived, King Solomon, warns: *"Catch all the foxes, those little foxes, before they ruin the vineyard of love, for the grapevines are blossoming"* (Song of Solomon 2:15 NLT). There is a threat to every marriage if due care and maintenance is not taken. Many people make the unwise assumption that their marriage is not under threat. Well, every marriage is under threat, according to the divorce statistics. In order to counteract a terrorist attack, it is important to be aware that there are terrorists out there who do not subscribe to your way of living. In the same manner, it is critical that every married couple understands that there are forces, environments, people and situations that are not enthusiastic cheerleaders of your wonderful, seemingly picturesque marriage. External threats can involve things such as ex-relationships, extra-marital affairs, pornography, and emotional involvement with third parties. To eliminate threats you must both work on ensuring your marriage is watertight, and a safe place where both parties can be vulnerable and expressive of their wins and weaknesses.

Counteract threats by identifying potential and present threats around you. Are there people in your lives that could pose a possible threat to the health of your marriage? Are there friendships, and situations at work, or even at church where the authenticity of your marriage can be threatened?

Trust is essential to the health of every marriage, and allows for openness and security. This inversely leads to a marriage that allows regular analysis and health checks to ensure you both enjoy the marriage of your dreams. Start to get active in safeguarding and analysing your Green Stage, by enhancing and promoting the identified strengths, minimising weaknesses, exploiting every opportunity available to strengthen the relationship, and making intentional, strategic moves together to eliminate all perceived, potential and real threats.

Scripture summarises the Green stage like this:

Ecclesiastes 4:9-12 (NLT)

"Two people are better off than one, for they can help each other succeed. If one person falls, the other can reach out and help. But someone who falls alone is in real trouble. Likewise, two people lying close together can keep each other warm. But how can one be warm alone? A person standing alone can be attacked and defeated, but two can stand back-to-back and conquer. Three are even better, for a triple-braided cord is not easily broken."

Being in sync together, keeping God in the equation and staying mindful of all the things discussed are required to maintain equilibrium in your home and can help make the Green stage of your relationship, heaven on earth.

Pre-Stage

A NOTE
TO SINGLETONS…

So many people around the world are ready to give up their right arm to get out of their season of singleness. Singletons must understand that there are many people in unhappy, painful, life draining relationships, and so many people are unprepared for a relationship. It is critical to your long-term happiness, and fulfilment in relationships to utilise the current status of a singleton to intentionally prepare yourself for your future spouse, and love yourself in such a way that you are lovable. It has often been said, 'once you learn to accept and love yourself, it makes it so much easier for others to love you.' There is a wonderful glow on a man or woman who has learned to love themselves while they await their life-long partner. Moreover, if you read, internalise and adhere to the Red, Yellow and Green stages of this manual, it is very likely that you will avoid unnecessary mistakes, and be able to cultivate a fruitful relationship on the way to marriage.

There are great benefits to consider in being a singleton:

- You only need to consider YOU! Married folks need to consider their partner even when buying mango or grape juice at the corner shop!

- You have the time to decide what you really want from a relationship and how it would benefit you.

- You can pursue your dreams and aspirations without reserve.

Learn to appreciate the season of singleness, and use it wisely. Clients of ours have gone from being single with no prospects, to married within a year, you never know, this could be you this time next year! If you're single, find the blessing in it and embrace it while it lasts. To help you do this, our Pre-Stage chapters will examine the importance of internalising your self worth and explaining what to do, in the meantime.

Chapter Twenty-two

'BECAUSE I'M WORTH IT'

Over the years, psychologists and other researchers of human behaviour have observed that the need for security, self-worth and significance are amongst our basic human needs. Intertwined with these three basic needs is Love.

The reason why relationships are such a hot topic, why many chart topping songs are written about love won or love lost, why new dating websites are popping up daily, and why many people will sell their Grandad's war medals in order to be loved, is because, many people have attached their sense of significance, security and ultimately their self-worth to whether or not they are loved by someone else. "After all, if I find love, and I'm loved, I must be worth something!" This statement is an actual excerpt from one of our counselling sessions with a young professional lady in her late twenties. The need for self-worth is oftentimes the driving force and the instigator of much of our behaviour, and even manifests itself in the way we dress, the way we speak, the places we frequent and the overall way we present ourselves. Everyone wants to feel they are worth something.

Selone and I believe that we have all been created by a Creator Who causes us to be of great value. However, if our need for self-worth, affirmation, security and significance are tied up in a romantic relationship, and who we have on our arm as we stroll down the King's Road in Chelsea, this can be a recipe for great disaster. An untold number of people will allow themselves to be disrespected, abused, victimised, separated from their families and compromise their morals in order to be in a relationship that is consciously or unconsciously destroying them. In the great search for self-worth in a relationship, they actually end up broken, destroyed, betrayed and made to feel 'worthless'.

We have counselled many people who have traded in their identity and self-respect, in order to receive affirmation and be romantically associated with someone who we all know is destructive to them. When self worth is tied up with, or based upon how someone else makes us feel, or is determined by a relationship status, this is a ticking time bomb, with disastrous and emotionally destroying consequences.

Too many lonely hearts and singletons are prepared to compromise their authenticity in order to have somebody, anybody to keep them warm, give them the ability to tell their buddies about their new 'love', and finally be able to update their Facebook profile to 'In a relationship'

It is vital for people to love themselves before venturing into the world of relationships. Essentially, a person should love himself or herself first, embrace their own identity, and understand their own values, ethics, moral standings and self-worth. Loving yourself allows us all to avoid the pitfall of placing unrealistic expectations on others, or giving others the power to determine how we feel or what we think, dependant on their approval of us, or the way they treat us. On many occasions, the person seeking a relationship portrays themselves as a desperate guy or girl, who views the approval or acceptance of their desired partner or 'person of interest', as the fulfilment of their life's mission. More often than not, the 'person of interest' can literally smell the desperation and be either put off by the approach, or mistreat the individual who has shown them interest. Love and appreciate you, otherwise it's going to be difficult to attract love or know when someone that approaches you, is here for love or something totally different. Approaching a relationship with the confidence that you are equal to the person you're interested in, will save you a great deal of heartache in the future. This will also empower you to live your life being content, relationship or not. The way you see yourself, and more significantly, the way you treat yourself, will help determine how others, including love interests, will perceive and treat you.

Similarly, many people have tied their self-worth to their socio-economic status: their career, salary, their network of friends, whether they shop at Waitrose or Iceland, their postcode or whether they drive a brand new Range Rover Evoque or are navigating the London Underground system with their Oyster card. Even worse is when people tie their worth to the number of followers on Twitter, Facebook or how many people liked their latest Instagram picture! Before you laugh, and call these folks 'pathetic' or 'shallow', if we all took a closer inventory of our own lives, and the things or people that dictate our moods, and how we feel about our lives, we are all guilty of allowing the externals, to dictate our internal moods to a certain extent. In order to live a life that's satisfying and not constantly yearning for the approval of others, we need to reverse this approach.

Who we are on the inside, determines what is projected on the outside. When a person is comfortable in their own skin, and is 'OK' with being by themselves, without looking to things, people or statuses to dictate their life, they have a greater chance of enjoying new or future relationships, and finding fulfilment in that relationship. If you don't love yourself, you have determined within yourself that you are 'unlovable', yet you have an unrealistic expectation that someone out there ought to love you. A man or woman, with the understanding that "Even if I'm by myself for while, it doesn't make me lonely or unloved, because I love me" will approach life, and relationships, without 'desperate' (figuratively speaking) written on their forehead. Before you venture into a new relationship, or take a friendship to another stage, take the time to ensure that you love yourself, and see yourself as 'worth it'.

It is always the manufacturer or retailer of a luxury item who sets the price, based on their own valuation of their product. They will consider the research & development, marketing, manufacturing, shipping, storage, packaging, export taxes, the positioning of the brand, and so much more. If the customer doesn't perceive the item to be worth the price, they can move on to another store, but the retailer or manufacturer is not obligated to reduce their price to satisfy the customer who is unwilling to pay the full price. The retailer or manufacturer would rather wait until the right customer comes along and perceives their product correctly. Guess what? Someone always comes along and purchases the items at full price. Retailers and manufacturers of luxury goods use pricing to filter out customers who do not or cannot appreciate their items. Although, you and I are not an item (there is a relationship pun unintended in there somewhere!), we can, however, learn a great deal from the manufacturers and retailers of luxury brands. We must learn never to lower our standards and morals, in order to avoid being 'left on the shelf' of *Singles R Us*. Knowing your worth, and not being desperate enough to say 'Yes' to the first dude or girl that shows a little interest in you, is going to help you keep your standard in check.

Bishop TD Jakes coined the following quote during one of his messages, when dealing with singles at a seminar. This quote speaks so much volume, and I believe it can help those currently single to gain a right perspective and real encouragement, without literally 'cheapening' themselves and compromising their values.

"Just because no one has been fortunate enough to realize what a gold mine you are, doesn't mean you shine any less. Never allow someone to be your PRIORITRY while allowing yourself to be their OPTION."
T.D. Jakes

Scripture tells us that *'We are fearfully, and wonderfully made...'* (Psalms 139:14 NIV), this means that so much has been invested into creating us, therefore, it would be tragic to 'lower ourselves' in order to hear someone else say 'I love you' to us. Rather than trying desperately to get that guy or lady to say those three magic words to you, why don't you wake up each morning, look in the mirror, and tell yourself those three magic words knowing also that there is a Creator who loves and adores you more than any human ever could. Sometimes we simply need to be like David in scriptures who in the midst of upheaval made a conscious effort to '...encourage himself in the Lord' (1 Samuel 30:6 KJV). Lowering your standards for the purpose of a relationship will cost you more than the disappointment of a cheap date; it could leave you stranded in a cheap life!

Imagine what your life or relationships would be if you believed in yourself, and appreciated you for simply being you? There is so much in you, and so many limitless possibilities awaiting you. Go through the different stages of this manual at your own pace so you will be equipped and ready for true love when it comes knocking. Simply, allow the real you to STAND UP and be seen because, you're worth it!

Chapter Twenty-three

WHILE I WAIT

I remember what it was like being on the playground in primary school waiting to be picked for a game of British Bulldog by the team captains during lunchtime. Oh what great memories! There was always a sense of trepidation if you were not one of the first batches of 'Bulldogs' chosen. As you realise you are amongst the dwindling numbers of those awaiting to be picked from the line up, you start to get worried, and possibly even start perspiring, as you don't want to be the one who is told to watch from the sidelines as others enjoy this savage-like bucket of fun and bruised knees. At my school, we always had one or two boys who took the game a little too seriously for my liking whereby a few of the weaker kids ended up with Nurse Harrison in Welfare for the rest of the afternoon. Now, picture this: with only two of you left on the wall, you didn't care any longer which team you ended up on, as long as somebody picked you! "Pick Me, Pick Me!" That's what's on the lips of a lot of singles that we have had the opportunity of meeting, or coaching over the years. Many felt as the months, and years go by, that they were like a young child standing in front of a wall waiting to be picked for a playground game.

There is nothing more unattractive than a single lady or single man waiting around, complaining about their current relationship status and hating on their peers when they hook up, go out on dates with their new boo, or walk down the aisle of a beautiful church. There is envy in their emotional make up, which makes their search for love appear extremely 'desperate!'

Your disposition as a singleton should be one of excitement about the possibility of what awaits, and ensuring you enjoy your time of being single, rather than merely enduring it. Until you love yourself, you shouldn't have an expectation that your prince charming or sweet princess will burst through the doors and just love on you. You must learn to love yourself, enjoy your own company, have a positive outlook on life, and be content and confident with being on your own. Those who are unable to enjoy themselves while being single will often be found chasing the wrong types of relationships, acting out of desperation, making destructive decisions that either lead to a broken heart, great disappointment or even emotional or physical abuse.

Many people, who are waiting for love, have a misguided and oftentimes unrealistic expectation that "Once I'm in a relationship, or once I'm married, everything will be perfect!" **Although relationships and especially marriage bring great warmth and great joy, there is no point in staying miserable or allowing life to pass you by in the meantime, simply because you're not in a relationship.**

Don't wait until that special someone walks through the door. Maximise the moment, enjoy your life NOW! Life is for living, whether single or hooked up, you must learn to treasure your life, treat each day as a gift, and allow yourself to experience love from you.

Unless you have psychic special powers, or have a Prophet on speed dial, you can never be certain about when love will walk your way. Therefore don't waste your moments, be intentional about living out your dreams, chasing your goals, travelling the world, and be committed to living life to the full. Each day is a gift from God, so use this time wisely, and enjoy it to the full. Remember, as discussed in the Red stage, a relationship is supposed to enhance your life, and you are supposed to make somebody else's life better also. How will they buy into the fact that you are capable of giving them joy if you allow yourself to remain in a downtrodden and self-absorbed *woe is me* state?

There is a formula we've adopted, which acts as a guide in various areas and arenas of our life. This is: **Preparation + Opportunity = Success!** In order for you to enjoy a great relationship, and have something great to invest in your future together, be committed to making preparations right now, where you are. A great way to prepare yourself and live full during those seasons of singleness is to be actively enrolled in personal development sessions, to build yourself up to be the best partner or spouse you can ever be. You can also attend singles seminars, and pick up all the information you can attain, so that you're well prepped to enter a relationship. If you have been hurt or left broken-hearted from a previous relationship, or you are just ending a bad relationship, rather than jumping straight into a new relationship, use this time to evaluate and implement strategies that will help you avoid entering another destructive, emotionally draining relationship. You need to consider what went wrong last time, what changes you will need to make this time and what could you have done better. Use this time to prepare yourself, body, mind and spirit to bring the best of you into your future relationship.

"So how do I find them?" we hear you ask! Who knows? Selone found me in a house party, and she hated house parties and wasn't even meant to be there! Another thought is, that they may actually be trying to find you. Whether it's socialising, getting plugged into a church community, praying about it, and getting involved in various clubs or just simply doing life until the right person comes along, the main thing is to be ready, as opportunity can strike at any moment.

Perform an inventory on yourself using the table below to evaluate your habits, mindset, self awareness, self esteem, spiritual walk and any other areas of life that you feel could positively impact or negatively impede future relationships:

Self Inventory

	Habits	Mindsets	Self Esteem	Self Awareness	Spirituality
Current Status Example	I tend to shout to get my point across	I believe that all men are dogs	I don't really think much of myself	People say that sometimes I lack tact but I don't really see it	I attend church regularly to top up on my spiritual strength
Changes Required Example	I need to find other ways communicate more effectively	I need to explore the possibility that some negative ideas I hold may be untrue	I need to find the beauty and skill within and affirm myself daily	I need to be more self aware and consider whether there is any truth in this seeking to make changes to avoid hurting others	I could set time aside to study my bible myself and get to know how God sees me
Current Status (Please complete)					
Changes Required (Please complete)					

What three words would you use to describe your present state? (e.g. hopeful, doubtful, content or frustrated)

1. ....

2. ....

3. ....

How do these affect your ability to relate to someone else?

What three positive words would you use to describe your ability to care for others? (e.g. selfless, patient)

1. ....

2. ....

3. ....

If you could change one thing about yourself, what would it be and why?

What is your best (non-physical quality) and in what way would you sharing this bring joy to someone else?

Having the right perspective about your singleness includes appreciating and celebrating all the opportunities it brings. It is a fact that there are some things a single person can enjoy which automatically disappear once you enter into a relationship. For instance, when you are single, you possess the freedom to get up and relocate, migrate to a new country or a new part of the country, take on a new job with crazy shifts, go on a boys only or girls only holiday without being made to feel guilty or anyone treating you with suspicions, you can also spend time on hobbies or with friends. If you're single and already a parent, you are able to devote more time to nurturing your children and investing more time in them, which is time you will have to share once you gain a partner. If the partner is in tune and invested in your children also, (which is necessary, otherwise the relationship will experience constant conflict), you can work together to find a happy medium. There are great things that are afforded to people during their season of singleness, things that some married folks and people in relationships would give their partner's right arm for, or swap their mother in laws for in the blink of an eye.

We have also encountered people who, for the sake of keeping up with the Joneses, or for the sake of being in a relationship, will either stay in a bad relationship, force their way back into wrong relationships, or compromise their values and ideologies to keep a relationship. Something to bear in mind is that it is more beneficial to be by yourself than to allow a time waster to suck the life out of you and sabotage opportunities to step into a beautiful relationship that God has for your future. Remember, you can never make anyone love you, nor can you force somebody to respect you.

"But what if I have already messed up a relationship?" It's OK; you can start again. You may have lowered your standards, placed your self-worth in the wrong thing or been guilty of treating a partner badly. It's never too late to reassess your approach and start a fresh. Why not try inviting Jesus to be part of your life and the 'Third Stranded Cord' of your relationship? We have, and the colours of love in our lives are as beautiful and majestic as ever.

If you're single today, while you wait, grow and appreciate who you are. Good things will come to you at their appointed time.

So there you have it, the complex nature of relationships broken down for you in bite size chunks. Use these colours of love to guide you to a better state of joy in the present and future stages of your relationship. Red, Yellow or Green, invest wisely in love and see rainbows in your sky, forevermore.

REFERENCES

Beall, A.E., & Sternberg, R. J. (1995). The social construction of love. *Journal of Social and Personal Relationships, 12*, 417-438.

Bennett, N., Blanc, A.K., & Bloom D.E. (1988) "Commitment and the Modern Union: Assessing the Link Between Premarital Cohabitation and Subsequent Marital Stability," *American Sociological Review 53:* 127-38.

Sternberg, R. J. (1986). A triangular theory of love. *Psychological Review, 93,* 119-135.

Sternberg, R. J.& Grajek, S. (1984). The nature of love. *Journal of Personality and Social Psychology, 47(2),* 312-329.

Lightning Source UK Ltd.
Milton Keynes UK
UKOW02f0914101114

241384UK00001B/5/P